Memories of a C

Bernie Meadows

A family memoir for those who wish to improve their understanding of the English way of life and the English language

The author has made every effort to ensure the material in this book is accurate. Any errors will be corrected in future editions.

The book was set in *Adobe InDesign CS3* by John P. Frisby.

Printed and bound by *Lightning Source UK Ltd*.

Published by *Mospeate Publishing*, Mospeate House, Sheffield S10 9EQ, UK

ISBN 978-0-9564949-2-4 (pbk)

Foreign Language Study: English as a Second Language; History: Social history; Biography and Autobiography: Childhood Memoir.

To my wife, Pat, and all the other powerful Homertonians

Acknowledgements

I am indebted to a number of people for help, advice and encouragement, and especially to John Frisby, my editor and book designer, for his steadfast and unstinting support. Without his help the book would probably never have come to completion.
Thank you, John.

My thanks also go to Keith Scott for commenting on the book at different stages and giving me much helpful advice.

Thank you, Pat, John and Alex for your long-lasting and loving support.

Published by Mospeate Publishing

Contents

Preface

This autobiography has two purposes. Firstly, it tells the story of a lower middle-class boy who grew into a man of no great importance, but whose life may provide some insights into English culture.

Secondly, it provides a series of puzzles so that students of English can test their knowledge of English punctuation, grammar and vocabulary.

I have produced this set of memories especially for my Chinese friends in the hope that it will be both interesting and helpful.

Some asked me: could I provide some text for them to practise their ability to translate from English to Chinese. They wanted the text to provide some insight into the English way of life. This family memoir is the result.

The title refers to the fact that my name *Bernard* includes the idea of *bear*. *Curious* has two meanings which are both apt: it can mean *strange, unusual* and it can also mean *wanting to find the answers to questions, inquisitive*.

Bernie Meadows is a Londoner who studied History at New College, Oxford, following two years' National Service in the Intelligence Corps. He then became a teacher, a husband and a father, but is now a gentleman of leisure!

How to use and enjoy this book

The Memories in this book provide hundreds of model sentences. The *Notes* and *Glossary* sections also provide numerous examples of short English texts. These will help students to understand the stories without continually looking at a Dictionary. They provide plenty of "repetition through variety."

The **Punctuation Exercises** at the end of the book will allow students to test their knowledge of English punctuation.

Notes
Some of these refer to points of grammar, while others provide background information. Asterisks in the text indicate that there is an associated *Note.*

Glossary
An explanation is given for some of the most difficult words in each Memory. After each **headword** its part of speech and its origin are given in brackets.

I think that it is useful to notice the connection between modern English and other languages. Here are some examples:

(1) **to baptise** (verb, Greek-Latin)
This word came into English from some stage of Latin, but it was taken into Latin from Greek.

(2) **to derive** (verb, Latin-French)
This came into English from some stage of French, but it was taken into French from Latin.

(3) **maiden name** (noun, Old English)
Each of these two words originally came from some stage of Old English, i.e. the language of the Anglo-Saxons

(4) **to dredge** (verb, Old English?)
It is believed that this word came from Old English, but it's not certain.

(5) **operation** (noun, Latin)
This came into English from some stage of Latin.

(6) **grocer's shop** (noun, French, Old English)
The first word comes from French and the second word comes from Old English.

(7) **suffered from depression** (phrase)
This group of words is not a complete sentence.

(8) **the bubble has burst** (sentence)
There is a subject (the bubble) and a predicate (has burst).

Punctuation Exercises

(1) Each exercise consists of a text with no punctuation.

(2) Students can test themselves by providing punctuation for such an exercise and then checking with the original *Memory*.

(3) Some students may like to make a copy of a *Memory* without its punctuation and then test themselves later.

(4) Small groups of 2 – 3 – 4 students may like to hold a "tea party" in order to discuss an exercise. This would make them think about grammar and spelling, as well as punctuation, because all three can influence the meaning of words in English sentences.

Further Games and Exercises

Some teachers and students may like to use photos, maps, charts and pictures in the book in order to create new opportunities for speaking English.

(1)   A teacher or student asks a question about a photo starting with one of the words: "who, what, where, when, and why?"

(2)   One person makes a statement about an illustration. Someone else has to say whether or not it is "true" or "false."

(3)   One student thinks about something in a picture and the others have to find out what it is by asking questions. It helps if the word is written on a piece of paper before the questions begin.

(4)   *Substitution Tables* can help students to improve their spoken and written English. A short sentence can be taken from one of the Memories. For example:

My name	is	Bernard Randall Meadows.
Your name		Bernard
His name	is	Charles
Her name		Maria

(5)   Students can change a text by copying it out but changing it in some way. For example:

(a) change 1st person into 2nd or 3rd person: i.e. *I* becomes *you, he* or *she.*

(b) change the past into the present: e.g. *was* becomes *is.*

(c) change adjectives and adverbs into their opposites. E.g. *old* becomes *new* or *young.*

Students will obtain the benefit of copying out a paragraph of English while still needing to think about what they are doing.

Family Trees

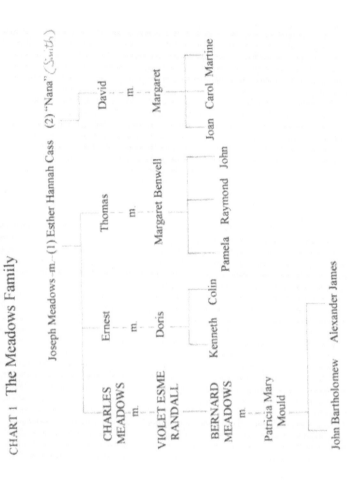

CHART 1   The Meadows Family

Joseph Meadows—m.—(1) Esther Hannah Cass   (2) "Nana" (Smith)

CHARLES MEADOWS
m.

Ernest
m.
Doris

Thomas
m.
Margaret Benwell

David
m.
Margaret

VIOLET ESME RANDALL

Kenneth   Colin

Pamela   Raymond   John

Joan   Carol   Martine

BERNARD MEADOWS
m.
Patricia Mary Mould

John Bartholomew   Alexander James

CHART 2 The Randall Family

John Rendell
m.
Mary Ann Trask

Edmund/Edward Oatley
m.
Amelia Webb

George Randall — — — — married — — — — Mary Henrietta Oatley

May   Cyril Randall   Rose   Henry   Edward   Margaret
          m.   m.   m.
(1) Lydia Hartwell (2) Alma   Elenor Mary   Kate
    Bishop Taylor   Ilett

David Randall   Joan   Roy   Joyce
                       m.

VIOLET ESMÉ
RANDALL
m.

CHARLES   MEADOWS   William Warner

BERNARD RANDALL   William Angela Christina
         MEADOWS

Chapter 1

BACKGROUND

List of Memories

1. My name

2. The meanings of my names

3. My father's parents

4. My mother's parents

5. My father's early life

6. My father's work

7. My father's brothers

8. My mother's early life

9. My mother's work

10. My mother's problems within the family

11. My mother's illness

12. My ancestors

13. The Randall family Bible

14. Church View, Dinder

15. My parents' first meeting

1 My name

My name is Bernard Randall Meadows. My father [1] was Charles Alfred Joseph Meadows and he named me after his close friend [2] who went to work for an oil company in Burma (Myanmar) in the late 1920s or early 1930s. My mother was baptised as Violet Esmé Randall. My middle name was derived from her maiden name.

1 My father Charles Meadows
He became a sound-recording engineer in the early 1930s and is seen here with a microphone.

2 Bernard
I do not know his surname but he was a close friend of my father, which is why my father called me Bernard.

Some of Bernard's [2] photos taken while he worked in Burma are still in my possession. One shows a smiling young man in tropical clothes with his shotgun and dog sitting on a car [3].

A few of the photos indicate that he was involved in work to do with dredging a large river – perhaps the Irrawaddy – as part of the operations of the BOC [4]. I don't know whether this was the Burmese Oil Company or the British Oil Company. It seems that he sent two watercolour paintings of the Burmese countryside to my parents for their wedding in 1935, but I have no idea as to what happened to him after that.

3 Bernard with his dog
This photograph of Bernard (second from right) in Burma shows him holding his dog.

4 Burmese landscape
This large vessel is dredging a river not far from a Burmese town.

3

2 The meanings of my name, Bernard Meadows

The name Meadows is not unusual in southern England. It shows that some of my ancestors must have lived on meadowland. According to the Oxford English Dictionary the word *meadow* comes from Old English, which itself developed from Anglo-Saxon.

A meadow **[5]** was originally a piece of land which was covered with grass. This grass would be cut and used as hay to feed horses. Later the word *meadow* came to mean any piece of grassland which was used for cows and other animals to graze on. It was sometimes used to mean a piece of low-lying, well-watered ground, usually near a river.

5 Meadowland
This drawing is based on the photo opposite which was taken at Oxford. It shows a typical meadow.

The name *Bernard* was introduced into England at the time of the Norman Conquest in 1066 and can be found several times in the Doomsday Book of 1086, but it came from Old German *berinhard* from *berin* meaning a *bear*, and *hard* meaning *stern*.

Randall can be a personal name or a surname. It was current in England as a personal name before the Norman Conquest. In Old English *rand* meant *shield* and *wulf* meant *wolf*, so *Randwulf* meant *shield wolf*. In the Middle Ages it became *Randal* and then became a surname – *Randall*, found mainly in southern England, specifically in Dorset, the Midlands and East Anglia.

3 My father's parents

My parents, Charles Meadows [6] and Esmé Randall [7], married on 22nd December 1935 at Bowers Gifford Church [8], near Pitsea, in Essex. This was the local church for the Meadows family and my paternal grandfather went there regularly every Sunday. His name was Joseph [9] and I was told that he had run away from his father when only 17 years old. His father had lived in Maldon in Essex and had been a lay preacher, but I don't know what his day-time occupation had been.

6 Charles Meadows, my father
Charles may have thought of himself as a debonair man-about-town. Note the handkerchief in his breast pocket and his cigarette.

7 Esmé Randall, my mother
Like my father, she also seems to have tried to be fashionable.

8 Bowers Gifford Church
This is where my parents, Charles Meadows and Esmé Randall, were married in 1935.

9 Joseph Meadows, my paternal grandfather, married twice.

My father's birth certificate states that Joseph **[9]**, my paternal grandfather, was a groom and domestic gardener. Although Joseph at first worked with horses, he was apparently one of the first pupils of the *British School of Motoring* and, having learnt to drive a car, he became the chauffeur for a doctor. He later drove lorries as a soldier in the First World War and later still he drove a van for a branch of the co-op (*Cooperative Society*) in Southend.

10 Esther Hannah Cass Esther was Joseph's first wife, and hence my paternal grandmother, but died in 1918.

I never knew my paternal grandmother, Esther **[10]**, because she died during the great flu (influenza) epidemic of 1918. Her maiden name had been Esther Hannah Cass. Joseph later married again to the lady I knew as my grandmother **[11]**. I called these two grandparents *Granddad* and *Nana*. I have no idea what Nana's maiden names had been.

11 "Nana" Meadows
Nana was the grandmother I knew.
Joseph probably got married not long
after his first wife had died, but I never
knew Nana's original names. Note the
monocle attached to her right eye.

4 My mother's parents

I also never knew my maternal grandmother, because she died on 9th May 1932 at the age of 57. Her maiden name was Lydia Hartnell Bishop Taylor **[12, 13]** and she was born on 14th August 1874 into a chemist's family in Leicester. She was presumably a middle-class person, but it seems that her father took to drink and his family then experienced financial difficulties. Lydia, who was also known as 'Lillie', became some sort of servant at a mansion in Dinder, near Wells, in Somerset. My grandfather, Cyril Randall **[12,13]**, met her when he worked there as a groom and they were married in 1907 at St. Matthew's Church, Fulham.

Cyril now worked as a tram driver and conductor **[14]** and so, just like my other grandfather, changed his job from handling horses to being involved with mechanised transport. Unlike Joseph Meadows, who eventually lived in a relatively rural area in Essex, Cyril Randall chose to move from the countryside to the big city – London. For a while he and his wife lived in Fulham, first of all at 15 Cranbury Road and then at 50 Rosebury Road.

At some time after 1908 he moved his family across the River Thames to 115a Aslett Street, Wandsworth. After his first wife had died in 1932 and my mother had left home in 1935, he married Alma, one of his nieces, and moved to 3, Colman Court, Kimber Road, Southfields, SW 18. He lived in this block of flats with his second wife and their son, David, for the rest of his life.

12 Cyril and Lydia Randall (right)
This photo must date to the period
of the 1914-1918 war.

13 Cyril, Lydia and Esmé
Cyril is shown here with his wife
and their young daughter, Esmé.

14 A London Tram
This photo may have been
taken to celebrate a special
occasion to do with the new
tramways. Cyril Randall is
standing on the far right.

5 My father's early life

My father, Charles Meadows [6, 15], was born on 24th November 1905 at The Cottage, High Street, Romford, Essex. He was a very bookish person. I seem to remember his telling me that he had read Dickens' novel *The Pickwick Papers* when he was only five years old. He was certainly more studious than his three brothers. Apparently he was offered a place at the local grammar school but missed this opportunity for an academic education, because he spent several weeks or months in hospital with some sort of problem with his digestive system. It may have been because of this that he was so keen for me to go to a university at a time when not many working-class and lower middle-class children went on to higher education. He himself continued to read widely and to undertake a variety of intellectual activities in his spare time throughout his life.

15 Charles Meadows at school
Charles is shown here (picked out with the arrow) with his classmates at their school in Romford.

Our family motto was *Try anything once* and this doubtless had an effect on my own development. How strange it is that the initials of *Try anything once – TAO –* can be read as the old-fashioned English spelling of the modern spelling of the Chinese word 'dao' , which can mean *path* or *way*. I was influenced by the ideas of Taoism while still in my teens and have followed this path to some extent for the rest of my life.

16 Chinese character *dao*
This Mandarin Chinese character was written as *tao* in the Wade-Giles system of transcribing Chinese pronunciation into English.

6 My father's work

My father left school at the age of fourteen, but I don't know what his first job was. I do know that he eventually became a sound-recording engineer and had at least one good reference from his employer. On 24th October 1938 the Manager of British Ozaphane Limited wrote:

"To whom it may concern,

Mr. Meadows has been employed for two years by this company as Chief Recording Engineer, during which time he gave us most excellent service. He is a most conscientious worker, thoroughly capable and full of initiative, a fact proved by the many improvements which he brought out in our Sound Recording System.

He was also called into our factory in an advisory capacity on radio, and here also he proved himself most valuable.

We had to dispense with his services owing to our closing down our Recording Department, and in the event of our opening up that section again, we should re-engage without hesitation.

I recommend him to anyone requiring his services without reservations of any kind, and I wish him every success in the future."

17 Charles Meadows, my father, with his books and radio
He was a bookish person, who, while still young, became
very interested in the new science of radio and other electrical
matters.

7 My father's brothers

My father was the eldest of four brothers. Charles, Ernest and Thomas were born to Esther, and Nana gave birth to David. I called my uncles [18] by their shorter, colloquial names – *Uncle Ernie*, *Uncle Tom* and *Uncle Dave*, but my father didn't like anyone to call him *Charlie*. He preferred to be called *Charles* or perhaps *Chas* (*Chaz*). Of course, I never, ever called my parents by their first names; it was always *Mummy* and *Daddy* and later *Mother* and *Dad*.

I have never understood why some parents want their children to call them by their first names. This makes the children no different from anyone else, as if they were outsiders. Only children have the privilege and pleasure of calling their parents *Mother* and *Father* or some equivalent words such as *Ma* and *Pa* or *Mum* and *Dad*.

My three uncles were all called into the armed forces during the Second World War, but my father had poor eye-sight and a squint in the left eye and so he was not called up. Another reason why he was exempted from military duties may have been because he became an inspector for aeroplane equipment not long before the outbreak of war.

My father, Charles Meadows

18 The Meadows family

On 5th November 1939 the Meadows family must have met together to celebrate Bonfire Night. We are standing in the garden at Pitsea not long after the commencement of the Second World War. *Back row*: Uncle Dave, Uncle Ernie and Auntie Doris, Charles (arrowed) and Esmé, Uncle Tom and Auntie Margaret. *Front row*: Nana and Granddad, Kenneth and little Bernard

8 My mother's early life

My mother Esmé was born on 7th December 1908 in Rosebury Road, Fulham, not far from the River Thames. She was Lillie's only child and had to do most of the housework from the age of eight onwards, because her mother suffered from rheumatism or some such ailment. Although as a young girl she must have found the housework very tiring, this experience served her well later in her life. She became a good cook and a capable housewife. Like my father, however, she developed a range of spare time interests.

19 Esmé Randall with pram
Violet Esmé Randall, aged four years, proudly stands with her pram, filled with dolls, in her back garden.

20 Esmé Randall at school
Esmé is seen here as part of a school netball team.

21 **Swaffield Road School**

This photo, taken in 2002 from a spot not far from her house in Aslett Street, shows the back of the school building that Esmé attended until the age of 14.

Esmé

22 **Esmé in her classroom**
She is standing in the back row, second from the left.

Esmé learnt to play the piano and passed several of the AB (Associated Board) examinations. She also studied the *Tonic Sol-Fa* system of learning to sing from printed music. I have her certificate from the Tonic Sol-Fa College, dated June 16th 1921. It states: *"This is to certify that Esmé Randall has passed the Examination in Musical Memory, in Time, in Tune, and in Singing from the Modulator* as prescribed for the Junior Certificate."* There are also two stamps which she later stuck onto the certificate, which indicate that she was a member of the choir which took part in the Crystal Palace Festival in both 1921 and 1922.

Esmé also liked swimming. On the 26th September 1922 the London Schools Swimming Association, Wandsworth Branch, granted her a Certificate of the 1st Class. (This probably indicated the first level of progress.) She also obtained an Elementary School Swimming Certificate from the LCC (London County Council) which stated: *"This is to certify that Esmé Randall of Swaffield Road School has passed the council's prescribed test in Swimming in the Educational Year 1922-1923."*

23 Esmé with dog
Looking more cheerful while playing with a dog at the age of twenty-two. I wonder if it belonged to her.

24 A thoughtful Esmé
Eighteen year old Esmé looking serious.

9 My mother's work

Although my mother Esmé had to work hard as a young girl and, indeed, throughout her life, she was a light-hearted person. She once told me that she had played the clown in class at her school in order to make her classmates laugh.

25 Esmé with apple at seaside
She looks very frivolous in this photo which was taken at Margate, a seaside resort in Kent.

Esmé left school in 1923 at the age of fourteen and I have a reference from an employer dated 5th March 1927 as follows:

F.W.Older,
Druggists' and Perfumers' Sundriesman, Wholesale and Export only,
*37, Walbrook, London, E.C.4 ***

To whom this may concern:

This is to certify that Violet Esmé Randall of 115a Aslett Street, Wandsworth, S.W.18 has been in my employment for over three years, leaving at this date much to my regret, owing to depression of business. During this period she has acted as Typist, Book-keeper and Secretary to my entire satisfaction. I have found her perfectly honest and straightforward in every way, and thoroughly reliable, and she leaves with my very best wishes for her future.

It appears that she then went to work for Gaumont-British Films in Regent Street as is indicated by the letter in *Memory No. 11.*

10 My mother's problems within the family

Some years ago I discovered some letters in a small envelope. They were addressed to Miss Randall, 12 Narbonne Avenue. It seems that my mother had left home and that this had caused emotional problems within the family. The first letter was undated but was probably sent to her at some time in 1931.

> *My darling Esmé,*
>
> *Will you come home? If I have said or done anything to vex you in any way I am sorry. No one could possibly ever take your place either in the home or in our hearts. I think you are persuaded by Mollie and if it were not for her you would never have gone. You know that you have not done what was right in this home for some time. You are out too much and just as I am trying to get better. If you will try and help us all you can and try to live peaceable, I will do all I can to make you happy. Come home. Ever your loving mother,*
>
> *L. Randall*

The second letter is as follows:

> *115a Aslett Street*
> *Xmas*
>
> *My own dear daughter Esmé,*
>
> *I wish you a very Happy Xmas. May God bless you always and take care of you. I enclose my little gift hoping you will find it useful and that we shall all spend a very happy day together,*
>
> *Your loving mother,*
>
> *Lillie Randall*

These letters are heart-breaking, because Lillie Randall died in the spring of 1932 and I believe that my mother felt very guilty about having left the family not long before her own mother died.

26 Lillie Randall wearing glasses
Lillie had this photo taken in Wells, Somerset, probably when she was still a servant at Sharcombe House in Dinder.

27 Lillie Randall with necklace
This photo of Lillie was taken in June 1931 at about the time that she was having problems with her daughter, Esmé. She died at the age of 57 on 9th May 1932.

11 My mother's illness

My mother Esmé told me that she had suffered from depression at some stage in her life. This may have occurred after her own mother had died. I have a letter from the Accounts Department of the Gaumont-British Picture Corporation Ltd., dated 2nd September 1933, which runs as follows:

Miss V.E.Randall,
115a Aslett Street,
Wandsworth, S.W.18

Dear Miss Randall,

Very many thanks for your letter of the 1st instant. I am very glad indeed to hear that you are now on the way to recovery from your rather serious illness. I am sorry, however, to learn that you had such a very bad time.

We shall be very glad indeed when you are able to return, as your services have been very badly missed.

The arrival of your letter this morning has reminded me that I received a letter from you some time ago, to which I should have replied. Will you please accept my sincere apologies for the omission which has been caused through pressure of work.

With every good wish for your speedy complete return to health,

I remain,

Yours very truly

Of course Esmé's illness might have been more physical that mental. She may have suffered from a severe bout of influenza. I have no way of knowing. Be that as it may, it is possible that her illness was made more acute because of the emotional upsets which had occurred in the previous two years.

12 My ancestors

I know very little about my father's family. I don't know whether Joseph Meadows was an only child or whether he had siblings. He may have had one or more brothers and/or sisters but my father didn't tell me much about his background. I can only assume that my paternal ancestors came from East Anglia.

I know far more about my mother's family, because I inherited the Randall family bible. This was given to Mary Henrietta Randall by her mother, presumably when her daughter married George Randall in 1880 or thereabouts.

I have the birth certificate of Mary Henrietta, whose maiden name was Oatley. She was born on 30th May 1856 and she came from Dulcote, which is the first village heading east out of the cathedral city of Wells, in Somerset. She was baptised on 6th July 1856 and died on 21st October 1945, aged 89.

Her father, Edmund or Edward Oatley, was a farm labourer, and her mother, whose maiden name was Amelia Webb, couldn't write her name, but needed to sign her name by making a cross.

I also have the birth certificate of George Randall. He was born on 5th August 1861, in the village of Merriott, near Crewkerne, in the south of Somerset. (He died on 11th January 1927 at the age of 65.) His father's name was given as John Rendall, a farm labourer, and his mother's maiden name was Mary Ann Trask. Like Amelia Webb, she also made a cross, because she couldn't sign her name. It seems that, a century before I was born, most of my ancestors lived and worked on the land.

28 Mr. and Mrs. George Randall
George Randall and his wife, Mary Henrietta, are seen here in a
photographer's studio wearing their best clothes. Mary, a devout
Christian, may be holding a Book of Common Prayer.

13 The family Bible

The Randall family bible has the following entries on the inside front cover:

Violet May Randall.

Born 14th day August 1881. Sunday morning, 3 o'clock, Redland, Bristol.

Cyril George Randall.

Born 20th day March 1884. Thursday morning, quarter past seven, Enderby, Leicester.

Amelia Rose Randall.

Born 10th August 1887. Wednesday morning, half past six, Croscombe, Wells.

Edmund Henry Randall.

Born 25th May 1891. Monday morning, 20 past 11, Dinder, Wells.

Edward John Randall.

Born 15th June 1893. Thursday evening, 20 to seven, Dinder, Wells.

Mary Margaret Randall.

Born 20th July 1896. Evening, quarter to seven, Dinder, Wells.

Baby.

Born June 22nd 1902. Sunday afternoon, 5 minutes to 4, Dinder.

When this baby died, Henrietta had just turned 46. It was her last child and she then lived to be 89. I met all the members of the family at one time or another except for my great-grandfather, George Randall, who died before I was born. Cyril was, of course, my grandfather and his siblings were my great-uncles and great-aunts, but I called them Auntie May, Auntie Rose, Uncle Henry, Uncle Eddie and Auntie Margaret.

29 The 3 Randall girls

The three Misses Randall may have been standing at the bottom of the garden at Church View Cottage. My Auntie May (the eldest daughter) is in the middle, Auntie Rose is on the left, and Auntie Margaret (the youngest) is on the right.

30 The 3 Randall boys
These three serious young
men were Cyril Randall
(the eldest son and my
grandfather), Uncle Henry,
and Uncle Eddie (the
youngest).

31 Eddie as a chorister
When he was a boy Edward
Randall sang as a chorister
(choir-boy) in Wells Cathedral.

32 Eddie and Henry in the Army
Eddie (aged 24 and seated) and Henry (aged 26) are seen here in a photographer's studio in Lahore, India, during the 1914-18 War.

14 Church View, Dinder

It can be seen from the Randall family bible that my great-grandfather worked in Bristol, Leicestershire, and perhaps Croscombe, before settling down to work in Dinder, near Wells, in Somerset. He and his family lived in a cottage opposite the church and next to one of the farms in the village. It was called 'Church View' for obvious reasons and I was told many years later that it had been built in 1589 as a hostel for pilgrims. Perhaps these pilgrims would have been on their way to visit Wells Cathedral.

I spent nine very happy months at the cottage with my auntie Margaret (see figure [35]) when I was about eight years old – from August 1944 until early May 1945. At that time there was no mains water. All fresh water was obtained from a pump in the back garden.

34 Dinder Church
This modern photo (2004) shows the view of Dinder Church
from the Randalls' cottage. On the left is the wall that I used to
climb up.

33 *Church View* cottage (opposite)
This old photo shows Henry, Margaret and Rose standing in the
front garden of *Church View* cottage. It was taken before World
War I, probably in the period 1908-1910. The white discs are
holes punched for storage in an old family ring bound album.

There was no inside toilet, but a privy at the bottom of the garden, and so a chamber pot was kept under each bed. There was no electricity, which meant that my aunt used a paraffin lamp for illumination, and cooking was undertaken in a stove which used coal.

Of course, there was no television at that time. The radio was run off a large glass battery the size of a car battery. This had to be taken to Wells to be exchanged for a new one more or less every month.

This was very different from my life in a suburban flat. My experience was perhaps a little like that of many Chinese teenagers during the Cultural Revolution, but with one important difference: I went to live with someone who loved me and in a village where I was accepted as a member of the Randall family.

35 Margaret Randall
This is the way that I remember Auntie Margaret, with her long hair and her kind face, although the photo was probably taken twenty or thirty years before I knew her.

15   My parents' first meeting

I don't know exactly when and where my parents first met, but my mother told me that they had met at a dance. It seems that my father had been impressed by her voice and way of speaking, by which I assume that he liked the way that she spoke the King's English rather than English with a Cockney accent. I can just imagine the scene:

> "Good evening. May I have the pleasure of this dance?"
>
> "Thank you. I'd like that."…….
>
> "Thank you. May I escort you to your seat?"
>
> > "Yes, if you like. I'm sitting here with my friend. Would you like to join us?"
>
> "Yes, I'd like that very much."

This meeting probably took place in 1934 or 1935. Esmé Randall took Charles Meadows to stay with her grandmother, Henrietta Randall, in Somerset in the summer of 1935. My father had already begun to make ciné films as a hobby at some time in the 1930s and his first two family films were put together in 1936. They were entitled *Leaves from our Diary* and *Summerset Holiday*. They included shots of the cottage at Dinder and of Esmé riding her bicycle around the local country lanes. This latter scene was given the subtitle of *Riding in the Tea-Tea Races*. This was typical of my father's sense of humour, because he was interested in the famous T-T motorbike races which take place on the Isle of Man and once went there to take some shots of the race on ciné film. Of course, the subtitle implied that Esmé was on her way back to the cottage for teatime.

The 1936 films also included scenes of their wedding in 1935, their brief stay at 115a Aslett Street, and their move in spring 1936 to Hastings House, Ealing. My father's third family film, *Family-arities* (familiarities) was made in 1937 and included scenes of their new baby – me, Bernard.

36 Charles Meadows
My father is shown here enjoying a traditional English cup of tea. I doubt if he often had time to sit and relax in a deck chair.

37 Esmé Randall in hat
My mother is looking quite elegant here with her necklace, hat and fur collar.

Chapter 2

EARLY MEMORIES   1936-1944

1 My pedigree

I was born on 17ᵗʰ November 1936 at a maternity hospital in Ealing, West London. My parents were English and so I am English, but what does this mean? It means that I am a mongrel, because the English by definition are not a pure race. Various groups of people have come to the British Isles during the past three thousand years and many members of these groups have intermarried.

The first groups to spread through these islands are generally known as the British and some of their direct descendants now live in Scotland, Wales and Ireland. Julius Caesar, the famous Roman general, attempted to invade Britain in 55BC and 54BC, and, although he was unsuccessful, the Romans returned a hundred years later in 43AD.

During the next 350 years or so a Romano-British culture developed and much of the population was a mixture of Romans and British. The Roman Army included soldiers conscripted from all over the Mediterranean area.

The Anglo-Saxons (and Jutes) invaded the land from the 5ᵗʰ century onwards and some of them probably married members of the indigenous population. After several centuries they had established themselves in what is still known as England (Angle-land), but they in turn were invaded by the Vikings from Norway and Denmark. Eventually many of these new invaders settled in various parts of the British Isles.

Up until now the only other successful invasion occurred in 1066 AD when Duke William of Normandy defeated the English king, Harold, at the Battle of Hastings. William brought a new language (French), new customs and a new aristocracy to our land. I am not of aristocratic descent, but I have no doubt that I am a mixture of British, Mediterranean, Anglo-Saxon and Viking blood (or perhaps I should say- genes).

1 Bernard as a baby
This photo shows me sitting on the lawn at Hastings House (see overleaf).

2 West Ealing

I have some slight knowledge of how I looked and behaved as a baby and toddler because of my father's family films. There are shots of me in a perambulator gazing in wonder at the cameraman . There is also a short sequence of me lying on a blanket on the lawn outside our French windows at Hastings House and of my father then picking me up and holding me up high.

There are two sequences taken of me later when I was a toddler. One sequence shows me in the local park toddling around and sometimes bending over to pick things up. The other sequence shows my mother and me playing hide-and-seek around the pram. At that time my head was covered with curly blond hair. Later it changed to being brown and wavy. Now it's smooth and its colour consists of shades of grey, although my beard is almost white in places.

2 Hastings House
I made this drawing in May 1998, when I was sixty-one years old. Our ground-floor flat is out of sight on the left.

3 Alma and Esmé
Esmé (right) is sitting in front of our flat with her father's second wife, Alma, at some time in 1937. Note the cigarette in Esmé's right hand.

My father added a little drama to the story of playing hide-and-seek. First of all my mother crouches down and walks around the pram one way while I go the other. She says "Boo!" and then we repeat the process. After this she sits down in her deck chair to read a book, but looks up occasionally, while I wander about on my own.

After a time she looks up and realises that I am out of sight. She looks worried, gets up quickly and hurries to look over the hedge which surrounds the garden. After this she walks anxiously in the other direction and then, as she comes back, she meets me clambering back down the steps leading from the French windows onto the lawn. Phew! What a relief!

3 Greenford

I have no personal memories of our time at Hastings House. At some time in 1938 or 1939 we moved to a semi-detached house in Greenford, West London, not many miles away from Ealing, presumably because it was cheaper than our flat in Ealing. This was after my father had lost his job with *British Ozaphane* in October 1938. The address was 29, Wordsworth Avenue, Greenford, Middlesex.

I don't know whether or not we occupied the two floors of the house, but I do have three memories dating from our time there, two of which may have occurred on the same day.

4 Greenford
When I re-visited Greenford in May 2000, Number 29 was on the left-hand side, but in my memories I had believed that it was on the right!

My very first memory is of an ice cream. My mother took me for a walk along a side road as far as a shopping centre. We reached a modern 1930s block of shops and on the corner was an ice-cream parlour with a curving façade.

It was a fine day, probably in the summer of 1939 and so I must have been about two-and-a-half years old. I can remember looking up at the counter and reaching up to take hold of the ice-cream cornet with the Italian ice cream already melting and running down over my fingers.

My next memory may have occurred immediately afterwards or the event may have happened at some time during the following months.

We were returning from the shopping centre when I noticed that a man was following us. He was wearing a Mickey Mouse costume which included a huge Mickey Mouse head. I hadn't ever been to the cinema and so the cartoon films and characters of Walt Disney were unknown to me.

The man followed us all the way home and when we entered the house and I went into the front room he came and looked through the window. I screamed with fright and my mother came running in to see what was happening. He was doubtless only trying to entertain me!

45

4 Our move to Whetstone

My third distinct memory occurred in March 1940 only a few months after the start of the Second World War. This was the occasion when my parents and I moved to Whetstone, North London. It seems that after leaving British Ozaphane my father was out of work for six months or so. My mother told me that they had lived on her savings while he undertook some retraining. This enabled him to enter the Civil Service as a member of the AID (Aeronautical Inspection Department). He became involved with inspecting electrical equipment which included radar.

He went to work at the Standards Telephone and Cable factory at New Southgate and so my parents decided to move to a flat not far from my father's place of work. The factory is no longer there, having been replaced by a commercial estate, but the site is about half-way between Totteridge and Whetstone station on the Northern Line and Arnos Grove on the Piccadilly Line.

Our new address was: 2, Victor House, Marlborough Gardens, Whetstone, London N20

My mother told me that she had chosen this particular flat because the living room faced onto Oakleigh Road, which was a main road, and so she would be able to see plenty of activity going on when she looked through the window.

What was my memory on the day that we moved from Greenford to Whetstone? I can't remember now whether we got on a single-decker or a double-decker bus, but I do remember looking through the bus's open doorway at a black cat, which was sitting on the wall next to the bus stop and looking at us. Did we have a black cat called "Sooty"? I think so, but I'm no longer sure.

Victor House, Whetstone
his 2009 view of Victor House shows a café and a butcher's shop underneath the
ats, just as in my days there. What had been the optical workshops on the left now
upplied hair-dressers and beauticians.

Whetstone
his photo of Victor House
rovides a good view of its
yout.

5 Whetstone

I shall never be sure as to whether or not we kept a cat at 29, Wordsworth Avenue, but I do know that we never kept any pets at 2, Victor House. This was a block of flats which had been built on three floors. The ground floor consisted of a workshop and two shops. If one stood in front of the flats, the workshop was on the left underneath flats 1 and 2. They made frames for spectacles and, on a few occasions when I broke my glasses while wrestling in the playground or the street, I was able to go downstairs and get my glasses mended (see figure **6).**

Next to the workshop, and under flat number 3, was a small restaurant which also sold bread. This was called *The Pantry*. My mother worked there for a while after I had started school. I remember on one occasion going into *The Pantry* after finding that my mother wasn't at home.

"I don't know where my mum is. Is she here?"
"No, love. She's run off with a soldier!"

I didn't know what the woman meant, but even at that age I didn't think it very funny.

Next to *The Pantry*, under flat number 4, was a butcher's shop. Needless to say, my mother usually bought our bread and meat at these two shops. Our flat, number two, was the second flat on the first floor and above us, on the second floor, were flats 5, 6, 7 and 8. Their front doors gave onto a narrow balcony, which was about a metre wide and on the opposite side of the flats from the road. Our own balcony was about three metres wide. A staircase led up to the two balconies from a side entrance on the left-hand side of the block. Beyond and below our balcony wall were the back entrances to the ground floor shops, which were protected by a wooden fence. Beyond the fence was a kind of courtyard with a set of four garages running parallel to the flats.

7 The garages
My parents are in front of the four garages at the back of our flats. Our garage was the one on the left—actually the third in the row.

8 Behind Victor House
I'm standing with Uncle Tom and Auntie Margaret in the yard behind the flats at some time in the early 1940s. He died in 1991 and she died in 2011.

49

6 Oakleigh Road

The Victor House flats ran parallel to, and were set back from, Oakleigh Road. This main road ran approximately east-west up a gentle hill for a mile until it reached the crossroads at Whetstone. Here it joined the A1000, otherwise known as the Great North Road, which ran northwards to Barnet and then led all the way to York and on to Edinburgh.

Whetstone was an important shopping centre for my mother. I can still remember the Sainsburys store, which was on the left-hand side of the A1000 as we faced Barnet. In the 1940s this grocer's shop still had a marble-topped cheese counter with large cheeses which were cut into pieces with a fine steel wire. There were several counters, each with its special range of foods, and so my mother and I had to queue several times in order to fill our shopping bag.

9 Whetstone
This view, taken from Marlborough Gardens, shows the left-side of the parade of shops opposite Victor House.

10 Whetstone
The parade of shops and flats continues eastwards along Oakleigh Road.

There was a short service-road in front of our flats and on the opposite (north) side of Oakleigh Road there was another parade of shops and flats. These were only two storeys high. What they lacked in height, however, they made up for in length, since there were ten shops under the flats.

Directly opposite our flat was a Confectioner's and Tobacconist's shop, which was run by Mrs. Carminati and her Italian husband; the latter died in January 1944. They lived in the flat above the shop. Next to the *Carminatis*, running eastwards, were a greengrocer's shop, a grocer's shop and then a dress shop. After this there were a hardware shop, a barber's shop, three more shops and then a fish and chip shop which included a restaurant. Beyond these was a combined petrol station and repair garage.

7 Our flat

Our flat was not very large. It consisted of a narrow hallway leading from the front door to a T-junction. The crossbar of the T was a short corridor, which led to a small bedroom on the right. This room had a window onto the balcony and eventually became my own bedroom. To the left of the junction was a combined bathroom and toilet, and then the kitchen, which was so small that it was called 'the kitchenette.' These two rooms also had windows facing onto the balcony.

At the end of the hall were the other two rooms, which looked onto Oakleigh Road. The left-hand room was our living room and the right-hand one was my parents' bedroom.

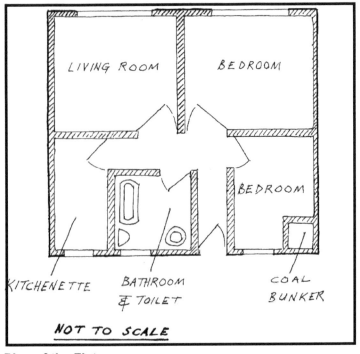

11 A Plan of the Flat
This plan of 2 Victor House gives a simple impression of its layout.

In the corner of my little bedroom was a coal bunker, which could only be reached by a wooden door on the balcony. This could be opened outwards after lifting a latch. Inside there were two or three planks of wood, which could be taken out if the coal supply ran low. As coal was put into the bunker, so the coal man would put another plank vertically into place in order to prevent coal from falling out.

I can well remember seeing the coal man trudging up the stairs and along the balcony with a cwt (hundredweight) sack of coal across his back and shoulders. He would position himself in front of the coal hole and then tip the coal in. It created a lot of coal dust, because he usually delivered two sacks of coal at a time. We needed the coal because in the 1940s and 1950s we used the fireplace in the living room to keep us warm.

12 Our balcony
This 2009 photo shows our balcony, and the window of my bedroom beyond the two wooden coal-bunkers.

13 My parents on the balcony outside my room
This photo was taken fifteen years after we had moved into the flat.

14 Rear view of Victor House (opposite, upper**)**
The fenced area is where the flats' dust bins were kept.

15 Modern view of the back yard of Victor House (opposite, lower)
This modern view shows where the old garages used to be situated
on the far left.

8 Coal fires

When I was still a small boy I used to wake up early in the morning and immediately want to get up. I don't feel like that in the mornings now! Nowadays it's more pleasant to stay in bed for a while after waking up. However, in the 1940s my mother didn't want me to get up early until she had lit the fire in the living room. We didn't have central heating and so the flat was usually cold in the early morning, especially during the winter months.

How did my mother light a fire? First of all she would use a small coal shovel to remove the cold ashes from the night before. This ash was wrapped in newspaper, taken downstairs and put in a special iron dustbin in an area behind the flats.

Once she had cleaned out the fire place she would lay some lumps of coal on the grate. Then she would crumple up some pieces of newspaper, which she put on top of, and between, the pieces of coal. After that she would lay some small, thin pieces of wood on top of the pieces of paper. The wood usually came from old fruit and vegetable boxes. Finally she would open a box of matches, strike one of them on the box, and use it to light the pieces of paper. The paper would make the wooden pieces catch alight and they in turn would set the coal on fire.

In order to help this to happen my mother would take another sheet of newspaper and hold it across the top half of the fireplace so that it caused a draught (a strong current of air) to rush up the chimney. This in turn helped to ignite the wood and the coal. It was only necessary to hold the sheet of paper in this way for a few minutes until it was clear that the fire was well and truly alight.

Of course, my mother was always very careful to see that the paper didn't catch fire.

16 Our fireplace
This drawing of our fireplace shows that it was in the modern Art Deco
style when we moved into the flat in 1940.

9 The chimney sweep

One of the disadvantages of using a coal fire to heat the flat was that it created a great deal of soot in the chimney. The vast majority of the homes in our neighbourhood, in London, and indeed throughout England, used coal fires for heating. From time to time a chimney would catch fire due to flames from the fireplace setting light to the soot, and this could be dangerous. I can remember seeing flames coming from a chimney pot on a roof on more than one occasion. Consequently, it was the custom for people to employ a man to sweep their chimneys.

My mother usually sent for a chimney sweep once every year. Before the sweep arrived she would take out the grate and clear away any ashes. The sweep would arrive wearing old, dark clothes and make straight for the fireplace.

Firstly, he put some old bed sheets down on the floor in front of the fireplace. Then he positioned a bag in the mouth of the fireplace. After that he took the top section of his brush which consisted of a disc-shaped brush mounted on a flexible bamboo rod. He pushed this up the chimney and, as most of it went up out of sight, screwed another section of rod onto it.

He continued to add pieces of rod as he pushed his brush to the top of the chimney until he could feel that it had come out into the open air.

After that he pulled the brush back down so that most of the soot went into the bag. He always looked very sooty afterwards.

10 Coal fires and fog

Another disadvantage of using coal as a fuel was that the smoke from thousands and thousands of chimneys helped to cause fog. London was famous in the nineteenth century for its fogs. Sometimes it was so thick that you really couldn't see your hand in front of your face.

Some fogs were called *pea soupers* because they were very dense and had a slightly green colour so that they looked rather like a pea soup.

The combination of smoke and fog also came to be known as 'smog'. Such fogs were a danger to both health and safety because they were bad for your lungs and could cause accidents.

Smogs featured in some of the novels of Charles Dickens and other nineteenth century authors, and that is why many people around the world still think that we suffer from them. Even in my lifetime I can remember several heavy fogs which made life difficult up until about 1963. Please don't get the wrong impression, however. We didn't suffer from them all year long; they only occurred a few times in a year.*

In 1956 the Clean Air Act was passed by Parliament to ensure that everyone used smokeless fuel. Many more people than before also began to have oil or gas central heating fitted in their houses. The result was that, for a time, there was less pollution and therefore less fog.

Of course, the pollution has not gone away; it has merely changed its nature. After the Second World War more and more people found that they were able to buy motorcars as well as motorbikes. During the past half century, traffic fumes have increased considerably, with the result that the haze that hangs over our cities is less obvious, and more frequent, than the old-fashioned fog.

59

11 Entertainments

Of course, there was virtually no domestic television in the early 1940s, nor had modern computers been invented. It was only after the war that many people began to buy television sets. Our way of life was very different from what it has become in the 21st Century. People had to undertake their own activities, whereas today a great deal of home entertainment is relatively passive.

I was lucky because my mother didn't go out to work during my infancy. As a result she was able to educate me at home before I started school at the age of five. She found the time to play games with me and to read stories to me. She also encouraged me to draw and paint a little after I had joined the local infant school. She taught me to play draughts (or checkers, as the game is called in America) and this helped me to learn to sit still, be quiet, and concentrate on the matter in hand.

17 Draughts
This modern photo shows a game of draughts in progress.

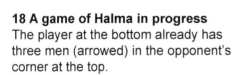

18 A game of Halma in progress
The player at the bottom already has three men (arrowed) in the opponent's corner at the top.

My mother also liked the game of Halma. I found this game rather annoying because it consisted of trying to make a bridge of your own pieces in order to get them from one side of the board to the other and was slow to develop. My mother was good at using my bridge of men to help each of her men cross the board to my side. She always won the game. On the other hand, I found that she could occasionally be beaten at draughts.

12 The radio

The radio also provided an important form of home entertainment. I can still remember listening to a weekly comedy programme as we ate our Sunday lunch. It was called ITMA (It's That Man Again) and provided our countrymen with a patriotic morale boost in the war against Hitler. Even as an infant I knew that the humour was very weak, but the jokes made us feel a bit happier. There was very little plot and much of the programme consisted of 'catch phrases.' Mrs. Mopp (mop) the cleaning lady would say, "Can I do you now, sir?" and an army officer, Colonel Chinstrap, when offered an alcoholic drink, would say "I don't mind if I do." There was also a German spy called Funf, (fünf means 5 in German), who used to say, "This is Funf speaking. I go, I come back."

The actors were assisted by lots of sound effects, such as the sounds of doors opening, papers being shuffled and things falling on the floor. These sound effects made the scenes come alive and helped to disguise the fact that they weren't really very funny.

One advantage of listening to the radio was that I could do other things while listening to it. Another advantage was that it encouraged me to use my imagination. A third advantage was that I often listened to light classical music without being aware that I was increasing my musical knowledge. It was only when I came to re-read my diaries that I realised how important the radio had been to me until I left home to do my National Service at the age of eighteen. The radio was never so important to me again.   61

13 My toys

Naturally, my parents gave me some toys and games while I was growing up. Everyone knows that toys and games can be valuable in helping both to entertain and to educate children.

For example, someone gave me a set of bricks which I kept in an old biscuit tin. I enjoyed using them to construct 'buildings' but it was then my custom to 'bomb' them by dropping other bricks on them until they collapsed. I suppose that this idea came to me because of my knowledge of wartime bombing.

I was also given a pedal-car which I enjoyed pedalling up and down the balcony, thus continuing my grandfathers' tradition of being involved with transport!

19 My pedal car
From the style of this pedal-car it would seem that my parents bought, or acquired it, second-hand.

20 Big Teddy
I'm seen here on our balcony with my mother and the large teddy-bear
which she had bought for me when I was still very young.

In England in the 1930s and 1940s it was not the custom to give
dolls to boys, but it was permissible to give them teddy bears. In August
1937, when I was only nine months old, my mother gave me a teddy
bear. She wrote in her diary, "Gave babe a teddy bear twice as big as
himself. He loves it!"

When I was an infant, these teddy bears were very popular, but where did they come from? Like so many things in England in the 20th Century they originated in the USA (the United States of America). Theodore (Teddy) Roosevelt was the President of the United States, 1901-1909. He was a very adventurous man who liked hunting bears. I seem to remember reading somewhere that he rescued a bear cub whose mother had been shot, after which an enterprising person began to manufacture toy bears which became known as teddy bears. Fig. 21

My mother also bought me a tiny teddy bear which was only fifteen centimetres high from head to foot. I know this because I still have it (**21**). My mother later made it a little pair of blue trousers, a red jacket and a tiny blue hat. She was good at knitting and was able to knit the costume in just a few hours.

21 Little Ted
I've kept Little Ted for sentimental reasons because he looks so cute in the clothes which my mother knitted for him.

14 Mealtimes

As I have said before, my mother was a good cook. This wasn't easy during the war because some food was rationed and all foodstuffs were in short supply. Nevertheless, I am glad to say that I never starved – except for one occasion when I was very ill.

Our family ate three meals a day: breakfast in the morning, dinner at about midday and finally tea in the late afternoon or early evening. Since the mid-1960s, however, I have used different vocabulary for my meals: breakfast starts the day, but the midday meal is called 'lunch' and the evening meal is called 'dinner' – or the 'evening meal'.

For breakfast I would usually eat cornflakes with milk. When I was given a boiled egg in its egg cup I would smash the top of the shell, peel it off, and then sprinkle some salt and pepper onto it. I liked the white to be firm but the yolk to be runny, so that I could dip thin slices of bread and butter into it. I know that some people like to cut off the top of a boiled egg in order to avoid burning their fingers, but this method never appealed to me. I suffered in silence!

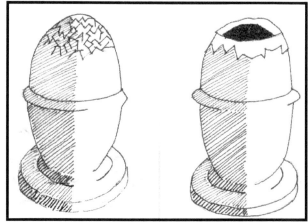

22 Two Boiled Eggs
The boiled egg on the left shows my way of breaking into it. The one on the right shows the top cut off with a knife or spoon.

'Tea' sometimes consisted of bread and butter with jam; sometimes it would be a cooked meal such as cheese on toast (known as Welsh Rarebit – or Welsh Rabbit as my mother liked to call it).

Sunday dinner was the one time in the week when the three of us sat down for a meal together. My mother invariably bought a piece of beef – topside – which she roasted for the whole morning. We ate this with boiled and roast potatoes and vegetables such as peas, carrots or Brussels sprouts. This was followed by some kind of dessert such as apple pie and custard.

There was always beef left over from the meal, and mother minced this up in her mincing machine. She then cooked this with mashed potato to make a shepherd's pie for Monday teatime. Sometimes she would use the minced beef to make savoury pancakes for tea.

15 Reading

There is a famous story, which may or may not be true, about the great King Alfred (848-901AD) who was one of our most capable monarchs. When he was a boy, his mother showed her sons a beautiful book and said that the first one to learn to read the book completely would be able to keep it for himself.

At that time, of course, books were very expensive objects. They were written by hand on parchment, which was produced from the skins of sheep. Alfred wanted the book and his mother helped him to read it, whereas his brothers weren't very interested. Alfred studied hard how to read the book and so won it for himself.

As a small boy I was similar to Alfred, because my mother taught me to read before I ever went to school. The NUT (National Union of Teachers) once produced the slogan "If you can read this, thank a teacher", but in my case this wasn't true. I wasn't taught to read by a schoolteacher. My mother read several books to me, one of which contained fables (i.e. stories in which animals can talk and behave like humans). I can still remember a picture of a bear wearing a shirt and trousers.

I also remember the first book which I read for myself: it was called "Teddy the Pilot". On the front cover was the picture of a teddy bear sitting in the cockpit of an old-fashioned aeroplane.

One day my father came home from work.

"Bernard can read," said my mother. "Look, here's the book."

"Oh, yes," said my father. "Let's have a look at it. Very well, read the first page."

I read the first page to him.

"Now turn over and read the next page."

For a moment I felt worried, because I had read only the first page with my mother, but the second page seemed to have the same words as the first and so I read that as well. From then on I became an avid reader.

16 Further reading

There was a series of children's programmes on the radio which featured Larry the Lamb and his friend, Dennis the Dachshund. It was called 'Toy town'. After hearing some of the programmes my mother took me up to Whetstone where she bought me two or three of the books.

They were not very big books and had a lot of pictures as well as plenty of text. The pictures showed very clearly that the animals were made of wood - as were other characters such as the Mayor, Ernest the Policeman, and Mr. Growser (who was always grousing). I loved listening to the stories on the radio and also loved reading the books.

I also remember a little book, printed on thin wartime paper, which described the activities of some fairies who lived in a mushroom house. I no longer have it, but I know that I felt quite sentimental about the story.

I can't remember anything else about the books which I read before starting school, but I still have my copy of 'Giant-Land,'* which my mother bought for me on 19th August 1943, when I was almost seven years old. August was the month of our school summer holiday and so I had completed my first year at Infant School.

She bought it from Barfield's Newsagents, which was situated half-way up the hill to Whetstone, when we went to pay for the weekly newspapers. The book had 250 pages with about 45 lines per page; the print was small with about 15 words to a line, and the vocabulary was varied and quite adult; yet I read it easily because it was a gripping adventure story about a boy of fifteen who battled with giants, and there was a full page picture every few pages. I still have it on a shelf in my study.

"Thank you, Mother, for teaching me to read!"

23 Toytown
In this picture the Mayor of Toytown is offering his handkerchief to Larry the Lamb.

24 Giant-land
In this picture from Giant-land our hero, Tim, meets Uncle Two-Heads for the first time.

17 Infant school

I believe that I began to attend a local infant school in the autumn of 1942, when I was well over five years old. Oakleigh Infants School was situated about three quarters of the way up the hill to Whetstone, and I shall never forget the day that my mother took me to see what it was like. We may have walked all the way, or we may have taken a bus from near our flat to the third bus stop up the hill, which was a short distance before All Saints Church. The fourth stop was just before the crossroads at Whetstone.

The school consisted of a long, mainly single-storied building and lay just beyond the church. As we entered the building I saw a small boy running down the long corridor. He was wearing a toy tin hat and seemed to be enjoying himself. The headmistress interviewed us and my mother filled in the necessary forms. After finishing our business at the school we returned home and I waited eagerly for the day when I could go to the school again – not as a visitor, but as a pupil. When the day came for us to set out for the school, my mother had no difficulty in persuading me to go. I was looking forward to receiving my own tin hat so that I, too, could run happily along the corridor. However, I never did get a tin hat given to me by the school and so I never did get to run along the corridor.

25 Oakleigh Infants School In 2009

18 Wartime education

I was never given a toy tin hat by the school, but I was provided with a gas mask. By the time that I started school in 1942 a great many London children had been evacuated to the countryside in order to avoid the heavy bombing.

The government was worried that the enemy might use gas against the civilian population and so all members of the public, adults and children, were provided with gas masks. The teachers and children at Oakleigh Infants School were required to practise putting on these gas masks and I remember that it was an unpleasant experience.

The masks were meant to be attractive and I seem to remember that mine looked like Mickey Mouse, but their appearance was not enough to remove their claustrophobic quality.

Naturally, the mask had to fit my head tightly and this was somewhat painful. As soon as I had put it on, I found it difficult to breathe normally and so thought that I was going to suffocate. I had to fight hard to prevent myself from panicking. It was fortunate that we never had to use them in earnest.

Sometimes there would be an air-raid warning and we would have to leave the school building and make our way to the air-raid shelters which were at the edge of the playground. Each of us had his or her own slate (a wooden frame holding a thin piece of this blue-grey rock) on which we could write with a piece of chalk, and we continued our lessons in a damp and dismal atmosphere.

I don't remember a bomb ever falling in my vicinity during the time that we were expecting an air raid, either in the daytime or at night, but I do remember that I was sometimes frightened.

19 Wartime classrooms

My first classroom was light and airy, but the desks were still old-fashioned. Each desk was attached to a bench which could seat several small pupils. In order to sit down at the desk we first had to raise the bench which folded up towards the back rest. The pupils would file into the space which was left and then sit down together so that the bench returned to its horizontal position. Individual cinema and theatre seats in England still fold up and down in a similar way.

I can't remember very much about my lessons. I do remember that on one occasion, at some time in my first two years, we were given a book about Robin Hood and told to copy out the first page. Robin Hood is a famous character in English fiction.

It was said that Robin Hood lived in Sherwood Forest, Nottinghamshire, at the end of the 13th century, and that he was an outlaw who stole from the rich to give to the poor. I wrote the page out at great speed so that I could continue to read the story, which commenced by describing a forest glade into which some horsemen were riding. Needless to say, I didn't manage to read much beyond the second page and, as far as I know, I never saw that particular book again.

I also remember that, at one stage, we were given matchsticks to help us to understand the idea of borrowing ten when we were doing subtraction ('take away sums').

After that I never had any difficulty with arithmetic, but I only learned my multiplication tables by heart up to 5x12=60 ("Five twelves are sixty") before I left the infant school in 1944. Even now I need to stop and think about any combination that comes after this, although I know, of course, that 12x12=144 ("Twelve twelves are a hundred and forty-four").

26 Infant School – my class
I believe that the Headmistress is on the right and my class-teacher is at the far left of the fourth row. I am fourth from the left in the third row.

20 More about wartime education

To the best of my knowledge our infant school teachers didn't make a deliberate attempt to entertain us: we went to school in order to work. Nevertheless, some of the lessons were naturally more enjoyable than others. I enjoyed the painting classes where we used brightly coloured powder paints in metal tubs – the green was particularly vivid – and poster paints in glass pots. There was one teacher who produced beautifully coloured pictures in chalk on her blackboard.

We also had music lessons in which a teacher played the piano so that we could sing folk songs, Christmas carols and other pieces. I took singing for granted from an early age.

I can truly say that I enjoyed school from the very beginning – except for one thing: school dinners. I found them to be very unappetizing. The vegetables tended to be watery and the meat was very unpleasant. Sometimes we were given mutton which was coated with yellow fat. I found that it was impossible to swallow it, because, as it touched my throat, I automatically gagged as a reflex action, although I never actually vomited.

On one occasion my mother came up to collect me at the end of afternoon school and discovered me sitting in front of a plate of food, which I was refusing to eat.

"Bernard refuses to eat his dinner," said one of the dinner ladies.

"Of course he won't eat it," said my mother. "It's stone cold!"
My mother took me home and for some years after that we had a morning routine as I left for school:

"Bye, bye, darling. Be good and try to eat up your dinner!"
        "Yes, mummy, I'll do my best!"

21 Some childhood ailments

I'm glad to say that I was not affected very much by the war, although some bombs did land in our area. I was more affected by the normal childhood ailments from which most children suffered at that time. My mother's diary for 1st September 1943 (1.9.43) has the entry: "Bernard home with tonsillitis."

Several months later, on 4th June 1944 (4.6.44), she noted that I had German measles (rubella). These illnesses were quite serious: they affected me so strongly that, not only was I confined to bed for several days, but I also suffered from delirium for some of the time. This was a strange experience, because my perception of the world around me became distorted and even frightening.

I remember one occasion when I was in my parents' double bed during the daytime. My mother came and sat on the eiderdown which covered the bed; I could see clearly that she was sitting beside me on the bed and yet she was also sitting on the wing of an old-fashioned aeroplane!

27 Delirium Plane
Here is my impression of mother and me on an aeroplane and our bed at the same time.

"Be careful that you don't fall off the wing," I said.

"Yes, I'll be careful, dear."

It seems that it is possible to have conflicting sensations when you are delirious. It is rather like seeing the two pictures in an optical illusion at the same time, which is not normally possible. It is also possible to experience a strange feeling of dread. On several occasions, when I was in the little bedroom, there seemed to be an evil entity in the room and I usually had to call out for my mother, but I couldn't explain what was wrong. I have never taken a single drug in my life, except for a few cigarettes when I was a teenager. Who needs drugs when you have experienced delirium?

22 Air raids at night

I have said that I was not badly affected by the war. Nevertheless there were times when the war impinged on my life. There were periods when we needed to go down to the air-raid shelter several nights in a row.

The shelter had been built on a grassy plot which lay between our block of flats and the road. I believe that it was built of bricks and concrete and had a rounded roof, so that it looked like a tunnel which was half-way out of the ground. It couldn't provide protection against the direct hit from a bomb, but it was far safer than staying in our flat.

At some time during the night we would hear the air-raid warning, which was produced by a siren fitted high up on a local building. When my parents heard the air-raid siren, my mother would wake me up, wrap me in a blanket and take me down to the shelter, accompanied by my father.

The atmosphere was cold, damp and somewhat smelly. There were slatted wooden beds with one above another. I'm not sure, but there may even have been three tiers of beds. We made ourselves as comfortable as possible and tried to sleep.

Later, when the siren signalled the 'All clear,' we would drag ourselves upstairs and back into our cosy beds.

23 A train journey

Our domestic life wasn't completely restricted even though there was a war on. On one occasion my mother took me to see my father's relatives at Pitsea, in Essex. We went by train and I can still remember two episodes from that journey. My mother's diary indicates that we left for Pitsea on 17th April 1943 (17.4.43). Her actual words were: "Went to Pitsea with Bernard. All round Tilbury."

Our difficulties began even before we reached the train. We stood in a queue for what seemed a very long time before my mother was able to speak to the ticket clerk.

"Return tickets for an adult and child to Pitsea Station, please."

"You're in the wrong queue. You must queue again over there," said the clerk, pointing to another counter.

"There's one born every minute," said a man standing near us*.

"Don't you talk to my mummy like that," I shouted.

Even at the age of six and a half I realised that it was unlikely for a grown man to hit a little boy like me, even though he was insensitive enough to suggest that my mother was a fool.

Once we had boarded the train our journey continued to be slow. Instead of heading east out of London we travelled south-eastwards towards the docks at Tilbury and then round towards Pitsea. We stopped several times, perhaps because of air raids. It was agonisingly slow, because after a while I wanted to go to the toilet, and our carriage had no corridor. We couldn't leave our compartment and therefore there were no toilet facilities.

I can't remember how we solved the problem, but I was very relieved when we finally reached my grandparents' bungalow!

24 My cousin Ken and a near tragedy

My Uncle Ernie had a son, Kenneth, who was a few years older than me. Four months after my mother and I had seen him at Pitsea my cousin Ken came to North London to stay with us for a couple of days. He was very good at making things with Plasticine (modelling clay) and I can still remember that he made a very impressive little warship - a destroyer about fifteen centimetres long and beautifully made out of grey Plasticine, so that it looked very realistic to my young and inexperienced eyes. Fig. 28

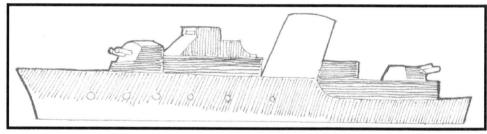

28 Destroyer
My cousin Ken's model destroyer looked something like this.

While he was with us something happened which showed that enemy bombers were not the only dangers in my life. My mother's diary has the following entry for 17th August 1943: "Took Ken and Bernard to Swimming Pool." This laconic comment doesn't give a hint of what could have become a tragedy at Finchley Open-Air Swimming Pool. It was a hot, sunny day and after changing into our swimming trunks Ken and I made our way to the swimming pool which was used by small children. My mother was watching us from the side of the pool near a slide which went down to just above the water. It was agreed that I should slide down into the water and that Ken would catch me.

I joined the short queue of children and climbed up the steps leading to the little platform at the top of the slide. When it was my turn I sat down with my legs over the top of the slide and waited for Ken to come to the bottom. I could see him beneath me and over to my right as I waited patiently. The girl behind me was not so patient.

She pushed me and I slid quickly down into the water and sank to the bottom. What a strange experience it was! I wasn't frightened but knew that I could drown and so I began to walk along the bottom of the pool towards my cousin. Perhaps the weight of my head prevented me from rising. Be that as it may, Ken lifted me out of the water just in time!

29 Swimming Pool
Here is a simple impression of Finchley Open-air Swimming Pool in August 1943. The children's pool and slide were at this end of the main pool, but are out-of-sight in this drawing.

25 Cinema and theatre

Reading books and listening to the radio were two of my most important pastimes during the war years, but we were also able to enjoy public entertainments such as going to the cinema and the theatre. The first reference to seeing a film in my mother's diaries was on 10th April 1943 (10.4.43): "Went to pictures with Bernard." This may have been the cartoon (animated) film *Bambi* by Walt Disney, which was about a baby deer. I have always been a sentimental person and I'm sure that I cried in the sad parts of the film.

According to her diary my mother also took me to see *Cinderella*, *Snow White* and *Mother Goose* during January 1944. I firmly believe that *Snow White* was the famous Walt Disney film about the princess, the seven dwarves who helped her, and her wicked stepmother.

I also have no doubt that *Mother Goose* was a pantomime which we saw at a local theatre—probably the Wood Green Empire, about three miles (four or five kilometres) from our flat. I'm not so sure about *Cinderella*; it could have been another pantomime, but it was probably another Walt Disney film. It has long been the custom to stage pantomimes in the Christmas period (December) and into January and February each year.

What is a pantomime? At its best it's a wonderful combination of acting, singing and dancing based on a simple fairy tale or folk story. It is meant to give pleasure to all ages and so it includes at least one comic character who tells jokes. The children in the audience are encouraged to shout out from time to time and therefore take part in the performance. The actors' costumes, the lighting and the stage sets are often beautiful. So are the legs of the female dancers and of one of the heroes who is usually a young woman, more or less dressed as a man. I always fell in love with one of them!

26 Our local cinemas

For one reason or another my father never took my mother to the pictures and so I used to accompany her to the cinema from an early age. This continued until I was a teenager and only ceased when I left school and entered the army for my National Service.

There were at least five cinemas within three miles (five kilometres) of our flat and my mother and I were in the habit of visiting four of them.

The *Ritz*, on Bowes Road, was the easiest to reach because we merely had to cross the road to a nearby bus stop and catch a 251 or 34 bus. The latter went eastwards past Arnos Grove Underground Station and joined the North Circular Road. Shortly after this we would leave the bus and walk back a hundred yards (90 metres) or so to the cinema. The building is still there but it's been used by a religious group for many years.

The *Odeon*, in Barnet, was also easy to reach because we walked a little way downhill to the nearest bus stop on our side of the road. There we caught a 34 bus bound for Barnet and got off at the top of Station Road.

There were two cinemas at North Finchley – the *Gaumont* and the Finchley *Odeon*. Both of them were reached in the same way: either we caught a bus to Whetstone and then caught a second bus southwards to Finchley; or we walked a few hundred metres up the hill to the bus stop at the end of Russell Lane and then caught a 125 bus which took us all the way to Finchley.

Going to the cinema not only provided us with entertainment but also gave us a sense of being in luxurious surroundings. Each cinema consisted of a spacious hall of modern design with thick carpets on the sloping floor. Like the theatres there was something magical about them and there were good reasons for calling them "Picture Palaces." Now only one of them remains – the *Odeon*, Barnet.

30 Ritz Cinema
I seem to remember that the Ritz Cinema had an exotic, Middle-Eastern appearance.

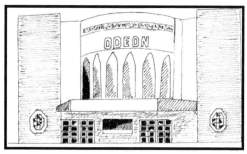

31 Odeon, Barnet
This looks much the same today as it did in the 1940s.

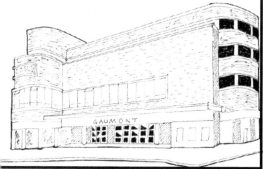

32 Gaumont Cinema
This cinema was very impressive when I was young. It opened in 1937, but its site is now occupied by a bus station, an Arts Centre and a block of flats.

33 The Odeon, Finchley,
This looked very modern when it opened in 1935.

83

27 My upbringing

As a child I was brought up strictly by my parents. On one occasion, when I had been naughty in some way, my mother put me on my parents' bed, pulled my trousers down and spanked me on my bottom, but this was the only time that she ever struck me.

If I did something wrong when we were in public she sometimes said to me, "Remember, you have to live with me when we get home!" When we were at home and she felt that I was being too noisy she would tell me to sit silently in one of our armchairs for ten minutes. If I didn't co-operate she could always rely on my father to strike fear into me, but I loved her and always tried to please her.

My father was more severe. Between the time when we arrived at Whetstone in 1940 and the time I left for Somerset in 1944 he struck me with a leather belt on at least two occasions. He may even have done it three times, but this ceased when my mother told him that she didn't like this punishment.

I found that being struck by a belt two or three times across my buttocks was very painful and I quickly learned to do as I was told. I'm not aware that it did me any lasting harm. Indeed, on the contrary, I think it helped me to learn to discipline myself and to realise that I couldn't just do anything that I wanted. Fortunately I was intelligent enough to understand that I was not the centre of the universe and that it was necessary to consider the feelings of other people.

It may be that being strict was part of the Meadows' family tradition. I believe that my grandfather was strict with my father and it is ironic that Joseph Meadows ran away from home at the age of seventeen. Perhaps this was because his father had been too violent towards him. The Randall family on the other hand was very gentle.

28 My upbringing continued

I wasn't spoilt in the traditional sense of the word. My father believed in the old adage: "Children should be seen and not heard." He didn't like me to contradict him and when we sat down at the table to eat our Sunday dinner (lunch) we didn't talk at all. Perhaps I became talkative at school as a way of compensating for this deficiency and, indeed, in later years a teacher at my infant school called me a 'Chatterbox', which became my nickname for a while. From an early age I was expected to conform to the wishes of my parents, my teachers and any other adults with whom I came into contact.

Yet I must admit that I was very spoilt indeed. As an only child I didn't have to compete with brothers and sisters. Although I was expected to be polite and to respect the wishes of others, my parents never interfered with my thinking. My mother brought me up as a Christian, but in later years, when I began to study Buddhism, she merely said, "Please be careful, dear."

Years before I came across the Taoist idea of Yin and Yang I was experiencing this combination of opposites within my own family and within myself: severity and kindness; sociability and solitude; conformity and free thinking. As long as I was polite and considerate towards others I was allowed to think for myself, and my school education encouraged me to continue this process.

34 The Yin-Yang Symbol
This is one version of the ancient Chinese symbol which represents the concept of Yin and Yang.

29 Charles Meadows and the Royal Air Force

In 1943 I was given a book about Poland which had been published by the Polish Library in Glasgow, Scotland. This is another book which is still on one of my bookshelves. On the title page was written: "To Bernard from N.C.O. of the Polish Regular Air Force, London 21.2.1943 (21st February 1943) W. Bodak."

N.C.O. stands for 'non-commissioned officer' – such as Corporal or Sergeant. Sergeant Bodak was a friend of my father's and I believe that they met because of my father's work in the AID (Aeronautical Investigation Department). Sgt. Bodak came and stayed with us both in February and in December 1943, and I imagine that my parents felt sorry for him because he had left his family and his homeland in order to fight for his country after the invasion of Poland in 1939.

I don't know what Sgt. Bodak's work was in London, but I do know that my father was involved in checking electronic equipment for the R.A.F. (Royal Air Force) and especially radar. He took his job very seriously and many years later, in November 1968, he was awarded the M.B.E. (Member of the Order of the British Empire) because some of his senior colleagues thought that he had played an important part in the development of aircraft radar.

Charles Meadows always maintained that this radar had helped to save the country during the Battle of Britain in 1940, when the German Luftwaffe sought to obtain dominance of the skies over Britain. It was effective radar equipment which enabled Air Force officers to send squadrons of fighter pilots to fly directly to where they were needed. I'm proud to think that my father's work helped us to survive in the face of possible invasion.

30 A new kind of bomb

In January 1944 my mother's diary has the entry: "Air-raid warnings," and in February she wrote: " Down to air-raid shelter." Again in May she wrote: "Air-raid shelter at night." Up until this time we had not suffered very much from air raids in North London. Now, however, a new type of weapon was sent against London – the V-bomb.

The first V-1 flying bomb was launched against London on 13th June 1944. These new weapons were popularly known as buzz bombs or doodlebugs, but they were not at all popular. They were actually long-distance unmanned planes, propelled by a jet engine, each of which contained the engine, a supply of fuel and a warhead. When the fuel ran out (i.e. when the supply came to an end) the engine stopped and the flying bomb plunged to earth causing a great deal of destruction.

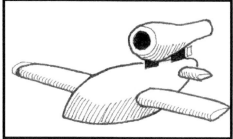

36 V- 1 Bomb
This is my impression of the basic design of the V-1 bomb. The 'V' stands for 'Vergeltungswaffe' which means 'Weapon of Revenge' in German.

35 Sgt. Bodak
This wartime photo of Sergeant Bodak speaks for itself!

87

No-one wanted to hear such a bomb, but once people had heard it in the distance they naturally didn't want to hear the noise stop suddenly; they wanted it to keep on going. In July we experienced these bombs ourselves on several occasions. At one time mother and I were at the bottom of Marlborough Gardens when a V-bomb cut out nearby (i.e. its engine stopped). I can still remember crouching down behind a wall with her. On another occasion one of them flew low over Victor House. After that we were on a bus at Finchley when a buzz bomb flew overhead. We also heard that four buzz bombs had landed at Arnos Grove and at Russell Lane.

These were the last straws!* On 1st August 1944 (1.8.1944) my mother went to the Town Hall at Friern Barnet and obtained the necessary evacuation papers for me. On 5th August 1944 (5.8.1944) she took me down to Somerset to stay with my great aunt Margaret in a village called Dinder.

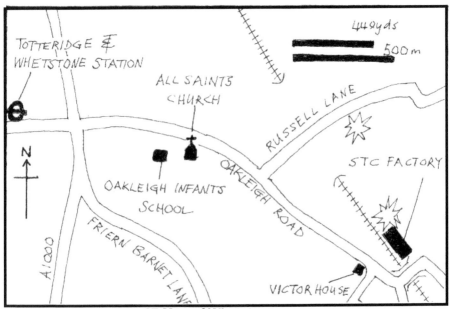

37 Map of Whetstone
The 'flashes' on this map show approximately where at least two V-bombs landed in our area in 1944.

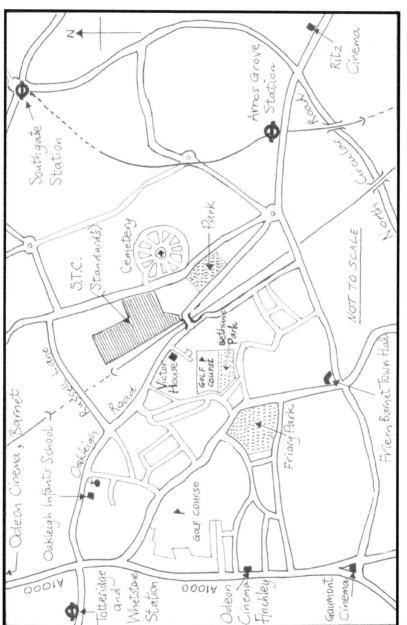

38 Map of a Part of North London
This map shows some of the places referred to in the text. It is not drawn accurately to scale but covers a region about 3 miles across.

Chapter 3

EVACUATION 1944-1945

1 Dinder's location

The last chapter ended with my being evacuated to a village called Dinder but I don't remember exactly how we made our way there. We certainly travelled by train from Paddington Station to Somerset, as we did not have a car nor were coaches available.

We probably went as far as Wells itself, because I have a dim memory of looking out of the carriage window as we left the Mendip Hills behind us and steamed the last mile across flat fields. On the other hand we may have gone only as far as Shepton Mallet, which lies a few miles to the east of Wells, but in either case we would have finished our journey by bus.

The bus used to stop at a countryside crossroads. To enter Dinder we walked northwards downhill along a lane with fields on either side of it. This was called The Rookery, probably because rooks would roost on the branches of the tall trees.

Then we reached a high stone wall on our left which enclosed part of the Somerville country estate. At the bottom, to our right, was the main street, which was called Riverside and ran alongside a narrow stream. Passing Riverside we continued up the slight slope ahead of us and then turned left into Church Street along the pavement which continued to skirt the Somerville wall. After about a hundred yards the high wall ceased and there were flowerbeds and gravestones behind a low wall and in front of the church, which lay back from the road. *Church View*, the name of the Randall cottage, was on the opposite side of the road from the church.

1 The crossroads at Dinder (opposite, upper)
This old postcard shows the cross-roads at the southern edge of Dinder. The Somerville mansion can be seen faintly between the trees on the left.

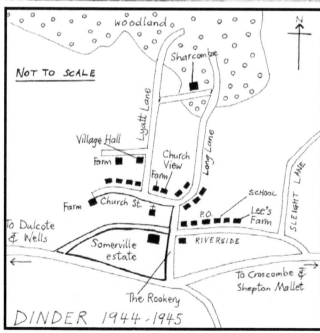

2 A map of Dinder
This is a sketch-map
of how I remember
the layout of the
village during the
period 1944-1945.

93

2 The cottage at Dinder

There was a narrow garden behind a stone wall at the front of the cottage. After passing through the gate on the far left of the wall a couple of steps brought one* to the porch and then to the front door. This was massive and the key was equally so. It was an old-fashioned iron key which must have been about six inches (15 centimetres) long. Naturally it seemed very heavy to a young boy.

The entrance hall, which was about thirty feet (nine metres) long, was always either cold or cool, because the floor consisted of large slabs of stone. There was a window on the left which looked onto the front garden of the farm next door. Halfway along on the right was a doorway which led into the living room and the latter's small window looked out

3 The house called *Church View* in Dinder
This photo, taken in 2004, shows what was originally a pilgrims' cottage in 1589. An older photograph taken probably in the 1920s is shown on p.105.

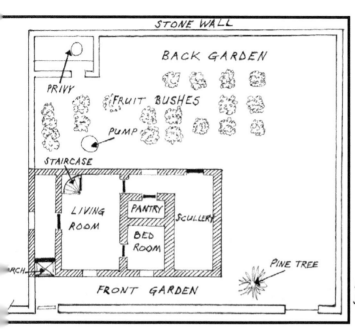

BACK GARDEN

FRUIT BUSHES

PUMP

STAIRCASE

PRIVY

STONE WALL

LIVING ROOM

PANTRY

SCULLERY

BED ROOM

ARCH.

FRONT GARDEN

PINE TREE

NOT TO SCALE

4 A plan of Church View
This shows the house, garden and outside toilet (the privy). In 1945 there was still no mains water, electricity or sewage disposal.

onto the road. A door in the far right-hand corner of the living room led to a small bedroom where my great-grandmother, Henrietta Randall, lay bed-ridden. A door on the far left-hand side of the living room opened onto a corridor which led past a pantry to a scullery, where washing and other household work was done.

On entering the living room from the hall it was possible to turn to the left, open another door, and then climb a steep and squeaky staircase to the bedrooms upstairs.

At the top one could turn right to enter the small bedroom above the hall or turn left to enter a large communal bedroom which stretched the length of the cottage. My Auntie Margaret had a bed at the far end. I sometimes slept in a bed by the door and sometimes in the little bedroom, whose windows looked onto the front of farmer Dyke's farmhouse.

95

3 Dinder's farms

To the best of my knowledge there were four farms in the village. The Lee family lived at the east end of the village just across the road from the small stream which ran along the main street, Riverside, and was as straight as a canal. I now realise that it must have been man-made for some of its course.

The Dyke family farm was next to our cottage and lay to the west of us. They could enter their farmhouse by walking up their garden path from our road, Church Street, in order to go in by their front door, but the main entrance to the farm was situated in a side road, Lyatt Lane, which ran northwards from opposite the church. When I went to collect

5 The Dykes' farmhouse
This 2004 photo shows the double-fronted house with its large garden. The farmyard was at the back of the house.

our milk, I left our gate, walked westwards for a short distance along the road, and then turned right into the side road in order to reach the side door of the farmhouse.

6 Church Street looking westwards
This road became a lane with a farm at the far end.

At the roadside there was a wooden platform on which stood the milk churns which held the milk which had been collected from the cows. Every day a tanker would come and collect the churns in order to take them to a depot where the milk would be bottled before being sent to distributors. Some of the milk would be sent to dairies to be made into butter, cream and cheese.

The side road was called Lyatt Lane because it led northwards towards a hill called Lyatt. I believe that there was a small farm on the left, but I don't remember the family's name. There was another farm at the end of Church Street at the west end of the village. There was a gate next to it, and sometimes my aunt and I would go through this gate in order to walk across the fields all the way to Wells. There were so many cows in the fields that I suppose that all the farms were essentially dairy farms.

4 A hot summer

I arrived at Dinder in the first week of August 1944. There was probably some rain during that month, but my memory is of a very hot summer. Although I was homesick for the first few weeks, the days passed very happily.

There was no work for me to do. My only task was to take the milk jug next door in order to collect the milk. The jug would be covered with a cloth which had beads hanging around the edge. The beads' weight kept it in place and this cloth served to prevent flies from getting at the milk in the same way that some Chinese like to have ceramic covers for their teacups.

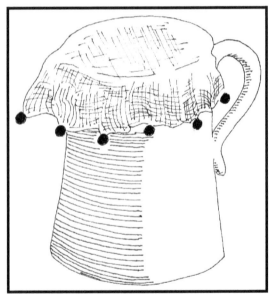

7 A milk jug
This was the kind of jug in which I collected fresh milk every day.

I would take the jug to the side door and ring the bell. The top half of the door could be opened separately from the bottom and was usually left open in the hot weather. The farmer's wife would take the jug and fill it from a milk churn using a large iron or steel ladle.

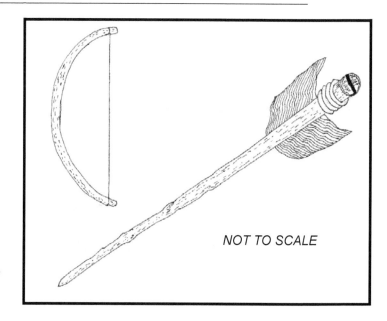

NOT TO SCALE

8 A home-made bow and arrow

What I liked best about my first few weeks in the village was that my playground consisted of woods and fields rather than the streets and parks of North London. The older boys made bows and arrows and then shot them into the air in the fields.

On one occasion I went to the edge of the wood with a boy who cut a sapling, trimmed the leaves and twigs off it and made it into a bow by joining the two ends together with a piece of string. He also made an arrow by carving a point at one end of a thin, straight branch. He split the other end and put a chicken's feather into the slit, which he then closed by twisting a piece of wire around the very end of the shaft.

It gave me great pleasure to fire the arrow into the air and have it descend vertically into the ground. Yet it could be dangerous. One arrow hit me on one of my ears and for years afterwards that ear used to crack and become sore in the springtime. It still does this sometimes!

5 Riverside

Dinder's main street was called Riverside. It ran approximately east-west and joined the Wells-Shepton Mallet road after about a quarter of a mile (440 yards). It commenced opposite a large gate in the wall of the Somerville estate.

As one entered Riverside from the western end there was a large house on the right-hand side. A Church of England priest by the name of Canon Burnell lived there and I believe that his residence was the vicarage for the village church. After this there were very few, if any, houses on the south side of the street, merely the narrow stream and then fields which stretched as far as the main road.

The north side of the street consisted almost entirely of houses and cottages which continued for about two hundred yards as far as the Lee farm. Shortly after this there was another lane, Sleight Lane, which ran northwards over the hill and past Dinder Wood, and then more fields. There was an isolated house beyond this lane and I knew the boy who lived there, but I don't remember his name.

The only other buildings on Riverside were Dinder Post Office and the village school. The school was quite small and the two women teachers lived on the premises.

I believe that the post office included a small village shop as happens in many English villages, but there was no public house. This is very unusual! Most villages in England, however small, tend to have a pub somewhere in the vicinity. Instead there was only an off-licence, where one could purchase alcohol to take home.

Just a church, four farms, two mansions and a post office in addition to the relatively few ordinary houses. I really was deep in the countryside!

9 Riverside
The railings of the village school are on the right. Dulcote Hill can be seen in the distance on the extreme left through the branches of the trees.

6 *Some open-air activities*

Once or twice I got into trouble with Auntie Margaret because I was late arriving back at the cottage after playing out in the fields with one or two of the village boys. At that age I was too young to understand why she was telling me off. It never entered my head that the world could be a dangerous place. Nevertheless, as I didn't like being scolded, I soon learnt to get home at the right time.

My aunt was acquainted with the lady who lived in the last house at the west end of the village and her son was about the same age as me.* We played together several times and I remember that on one occasion we played down by the stream which flowed through the Somerville parkland. I enjoyed being in the open air.

10 Church View and Church Street
My climbing wall can be seen on the left.

Usually I played nearer to home. A few of the village boys and girls would sometimes congregate by the low wall which fronted the churchyard and I would join in their talk and activities.

This wall abutted against (joined end-to-end with) a much taller wall which was about seven or eight feet high (two metres or so). This tall wall ran eastwards from the churchyard to the corner of the road and was topped by a set of flat copestones (capstones).

The face of the wall was very rough. It was made of flint stones, bits of brick and cement, and had been weathered by the wind and rain.

We used to climb up the wall as though we were on a vertical mountainside. We would then walk along the copestones as though we were on a pavement until we reached the corner of the road, where the wall was blocked by some kind of building.

Since then I have never wanted to indulge in mountain climbing, but that wall in Dinder gave me a lot of pleasure as I looked for footholds and handholds, and slowly made my way up the face of my own little mountain.

7 Food parcels

Although I felt homesick during my first few weeks at Dinder, I have to admit that I didn't miss my parents as much as I should have done. The reason for my happiness, at a time when I should have felt sad, is that my stay in the village felt like an extended holiday—even when the summer holiday came to an end and I became a pupil at the village school.

My mother kept in touch with me by sending me a parcel every so often, probably about once a month, and so it seemed as though Christmas and my birthday were being combined repeatedly every few weeks. She would send some sweets, chocolates and other 'goodies' together with copies of the Daily Mirror* and a letter telling me about her own news.

My aunt and I developed a game in which I would say "What's that over there?" and she would look round. Then I would snatch something from the parcel. After that she would distract my attention so that she could also snatch something. It was doubtless a silly game, but it gave us some amusement.

I also enjoyed looking at the newspaper, but I can't remember whether or not I read the news. One of the pages contained half a dozen strip cartoons* such as *Jane*, *Buck Ryan*, *Garth*, and *Just Jake*. I always looked at these and on several occasions I copied pictures of cars from one of the cartoons.

As well as sending me a parcel more or less every month my mother managed to come and see me several times during my enforced holiday away from home. Indeed, my father was able to accompany her when she first came down in September, but after that she came alone.

3 (Contd. from Memory 2 in this chapter) Church Street looking eastward
This old picture, probably taken in the 1920s, shows the house called *Church View* (also shown
in the modern photograph in Memory 2).

8 Walking in the countryside

During my time in Somerset I got used to walking along lanes and across fields. I didn't have a bicycle and couldn't have ridden it even if I had owned one. Our only transport was provided by buses; cars were comparatively rare. I seem to remember once walking with Auntie Margaret from Dinder across the fields all the way to Wells, but we usually walked up the lane and caught a bus.

On at least one occasion I went walking across some fields with my aunt who collected some edible mushrooms. She brought them back to the cottage and cooked them in a frying pan, but I didn't like them.

One of my favourite walks was to go northwards along the lane opposite the church, which led up to Lyatt Hill. This led past a large house or mansion the name of which was 'Sharcombe'. I believe that this was the establishment at which Cyril Randall met Lillie Taylor in the first decade of the twentieth century. Sometimes I would meet a herd of cows being brought back to their farm and I must say that I always found them rather frightening: they seemed so big and clumsy.

On one occasion, when my mother came to stay for the weekend, she and I walked from the cottage to a public house in Croscombe. It was only a mile away and took about twenty-five minutes, but it seemed like a long way to me at the age of eight. It was also a big treat for me, because I was allowed to drink a glass of cider. This is an alcoholic drink made from apples. It's a popular drink in the West Country and I was permitted to sample a small glass of the 'scrumpy,' which is a rough, dry and very strong cider.

In the past decade my wife and I have developed the habit of going for long walks in the countryside around London and we have also gone on walking holidays abroad, but I know that my love of walking in the countryside first began when I was an evacuee in Somerset.

Man collecting apples

Man holding ladder

11 An apple orchard
My father took this picture somewhere in the West Country.

12 Some apples and a bottle of strong cider
Cider can be dangerous because its alcohol content can be much higher than that of beer.

9 Dinder School

As I mentioned earlier the village school was located in the street called Riverside. It was built of stone, as were most of the buildings in the village. There was a stone wall around the playground, which was at the back of the building, and some iron railings along the frontage.

I seem to remember that there was only one large classroom together with a small hall and these two rooms were adequate because there were only about a dozen pupils. We had our lessons in the room and ate our school dinners in the hall.

I was probably one of the youngest in the school but the eldest boys and girls seemed to be several years older than me. Perhaps they didn't go to secondary education at the usual age of eleven but stayed on in the village school for an extra year or two.

I can remember very little of our lessons but I think that a good deal of the work was set for individual pupils. Presumably I was required to undertake problems in arithmetic and I remember having to do some writing, but my chief memories are of making a Viking boat out of thin cardboard and of having some help in making a blotter to give to my mother for Christmas.

At that time blotting paper was very important because ballpoint pens had not been invented and therefore people still used pen and ink. It was the custom for a writer to press his or her sheet of paper on to a piece of blotting paper in order to dry the ink after writing something, and thus prevent it from smudging.

Most memorable of all, however, was *The Hobbit*, which one of the teachers gave me to read. This famous book by J.R.R. Tolkien had been published only a few years previously. Although it was heavy going in some ways, I enjoyed it immensely.

13 Dinder School

10 Trips into Wells

In a previous 'memory' I mentioned that my aunt had to go into Wells every month or so in order to obtain a new radio battery. We would walk up the gentle slope to the bus stop, which was on the other side of the main road almost opposite the lane. Occasionally we would be lucky. Someone who recognised my aunt would stop his car and offer us a lift into Wells. Normally, however, we would have to wait for a bus.

Of course, I enjoyed these trips because it gave me a chance to see the shops. Sometimes we went into a café and my aunt bought me a vanilla ice cream covered with blackcurrant juice. This wasn't in a cornet but was on a plate and eaten with a spoon. Once or twice we went to the cinema, which was not always an enjoyable experience for reasons that I'll explain later.

Wells is famous for its cathedral, the construction of which is thought to have commenced in 1186. It's a good example of an ecclesiastical city which still provides some impressions of its medieval origins. Some people think that the cathedral is one of the loveliest in England.

In my opinion the West Front is an impressive sight due to several hundred statues which are arranged in tiers. There is a clock at the side, dating from the end of the 14th century, which not only tells the time but also shows the date of the month and the phases of the moon. The mechanism also activates the movement of some model knights which strike small bells to mark each hour.

Close to the cathedral is the Bishop's Palace, which is surrounded by a moat, and a bell by the bridge is rung by the swans when they feel hungry. Most people who visit Wells make sure that they see the cathedral, the Bishop's Palace and the moat with the swans.

Wells Cathedral

Archway over the street

14 Vicar's Close
You can see the archway leading into this very old street with Wells
Cathedral in the distance beyond it.

11 Cowboys and spiders

I know that I went into Wells at least twice in order to go to the cinema, because two films have stuck in my memory. One was about cowboys and the other was a form of Science Fiction.

I believe that the cowboy film featured Roy Rogers, *The Singing Cowboy*, and he made a big impression on me. I came home and then spent several minutes in the garden entertaining Auntie Margaret with what would now be called 'rapping'. I improvised a kind of rhyming prose, which was meant to imitate something which had been in the film. I'm sure that it must have sounded like drivel, but my aunt listened to me proudly.

15 A cowboy

16 Close-up picture of a jumping spider
Notice the large forward pointing eyes used in hunting. Courtesy Thomas Shahan.

The other memorable film involved a giant spider and I must say that it frightened me. I can't remember any details of the film except for the huge size of the spider, but I do know that it didn't help me in my relationship with the spiders in the outside toilet.

There were plenty of spindle-legged spiders hanging in the corners of the privy, so much so that for a short period of time I relieved myself by squatting down by the stone wall just before reaching that fearsome outhouse. I had no idea that some neighbours could see me from their house, which seemed to be barely visible a long way away beyond the other garden wall, and so I got into trouble with my aunt after they had informed her of my actions. After that I had to be brave and venture into the spider-infested building. I certainly didn't linger there any longer than was necessary!

12 Chatterbox

At some time during my infant education I was given the name 'Chatterbox', presumably because I was prone to talk too much. This nickname fortunately didn't follow me into Primary education, but on 5th June 1944 (5.6.1944) my mother bought me a copy of that year's *Chatterbox Annual*.

She continued to buy me the *Chatterbox Annual* for several years after I had returned from Somerset. Sixty-five years later, while visiting several bookshops in the Charing Cross Road, London, I discovered a copy of a *Chatterbox Annual*, which had been published at the end of the nineteenth century – 1889, 1898 or 1899 – I can't remember which.

I mention this because there was a very big, old book at the cottage in Dinder, which might have been a similar volume. It had no covers and some of the pages were missing but it was a library in its own right! Like the volume in the Charing Cross bookshop each page was covered with small print - probably font size 8 rather than the normal font size 11 used in modern story books for children.

There were lots of pictures, stories and articles which gave an impression of children's interests and the way of life at the height of the British Empire. I remember that there was a serial story about some children who were flying around the world in a biplane (or perhaps it was a triplane) with a man who was probably a professor.

The baby fell out of the plane and into the funnel of an ocean liner but I can't remember what happened to it after that except that it survived somehow. It was annoying that some of the pages were missing, because it meant that I didn't find out how a story ended.

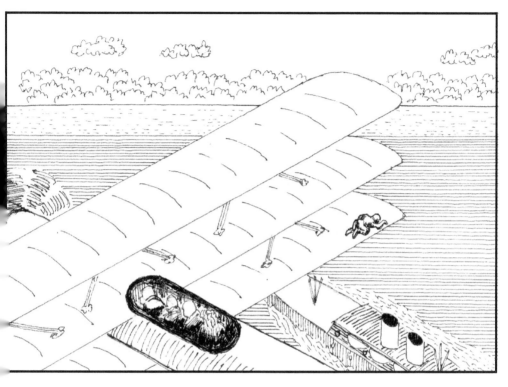

17 The aeroplane adventure
This is my vague memory of an illustration in the lovely old book which
I used to read in the cottage.

For example there was a fictional account of how people began to
develop arithmetic but the ending was missing. Whenever I returned to
the cottage after the war I inevitably looked for this book, but eventually
I found that it was no longer there. I suppose that it had been thrown
out.

13 More books

My parents came to see me for the first time during the weekend of Friday 29th September. After that my mother had to come alone, because my father worked on Saturday mornings and couldn't take time off work.

On that Saturday my mother and I went into Wells and while there we visited the bookshop which was on the right-hand side halfway down the hill from the town square.

She bought two books for me—*Rudkin* and *A Gang of Ten*, which I still have on a shelf in my study. They were both hardback books: their covers were a combination of cardboard and linen and I still think that books with linen covers are beautiful because of the pattern of the cloth.

Rudkin had been published by Frederick Muller in 1938 and my copy was a second edition from 1943. I know nothing about the authoress, Yvonne Wingfield King, but I really enjoyed this imaginative fairy story which included lots of pictures and twenty-eight poems.

I found *A Gang of Ten* more difficult to read, perhaps because its subject matter didn't appeal to me so much at that time. It had been published by Secker and Warburg in the USA in 1942 and was then published in England in January 1944. My copy was from the second edition of March 1944. It featured a group of children of different nationalities who came together in a town in California. They included boys from New York, Norway, England, Russia and Holland, girls from France and China, and there was also a young woman journalist from Washington. The climax of the book was reached when they tracked down and caught two Nazi spies.

18 Robinson Crusoe
This illustration is taken from an 1842 edition which was given to me
by Jim and Nasreen Saxton in 1973. It is similar to the pictures in the
Randalls' copy.

Apart from these two books and the old-fashioned annual I also
found a copy of *Robinson Crusoe* in the cottage. I enjoyed reading
this so much that I sometimes pretended that my bed in the big
bedroom was a raft or a ship and played at being shipwrecked!

14 Whist Drives

While I was living in Dinder I attended several whist drives. What is a whist drive? It's a sociable event in which pairs of players play the game of whist against pairs of opponents and change opponents at the end of each game.

We played in the village hall, which was on the left of the lane which led up to Lyatt Hill and I enjoyed it tremendously. Whist is a card game which can be learnt quickly but demands a certain amount of mental skill.

Each square table seats four players. The two players facing each other across the table are partners. One person (the dealer) gives out the cards singly and face down clockwise around the table. Each player is given thirteen cards and the object of the game is to win tricks.

Each trick consists of the four cards put down on the table by the four players. There are four suits in English cards: Spades, Hearts, Diamonds and Clubs, and the cards in each suit are ranked in order of their power. The lowest (weakest) card is the two. Then come the three, four, five, six, seven, eight, nine and ten. After these come the 'court cards' – Jack, Queen and King. Finally the most powerful card is the Ace (one).

Usually one suit is chosen to be the trump suit; this comes from the word 'triumph' and such a card can beat any card from another suit.

The player to the left of the dealer leads by playing any one of his or her cards face upwards onto the table. Each player in turn must follow suit (i.e. put down a card from the same suit).

If this isn't possible the player must 'throw away' a card from another suit or play a trump card. A trump card will beat any other card except a higher trump and a trick is won by the highest card from the suit which has been led or by the highest trump. The winner of the trick then leads to the next trick. I rarely have the opportunity to play cards but my enjoyment of card games probably started with my experience of playing whist.

19 Four of the top playing cards in Whist
The Ace and the three court cards (King, Queen and Jack) are the most powerful cards in Whist. These four are in the suit of Hearts.

15 Christmas 1944

For many English people Christmas is one of the most important times of the year. Christmas Day, which is always celebrated on 25th December, is the time when the members of a family eat a special meal together and give each other presents.

It is the custom to put up special decorations a few days in advance and these may include the Christmas cards which have been sent by other people. A Christmas tree may be put up in the living room and this is often a young pine tree, although artificial Christmas trees are also popular. A well-decorated pine tree can look glorious with its candles, glass balls and other ornaments.

It is still the custom to play games of one kind or another, although television is now also an important part of many people's Christmases. Many families still visit the theatre in order to see a pantomime, musical show or some other theatrical event and this is especially so on Boxing Day, which usually occurs on the day after Christmas Day.

However, I remember nothing of my first Christmas away from home in December 1944 except that it snowed and that my mother was able to come to stay with us in our Somerset cottage.

The snow may have started to fall after Christmas, but be that as it may, when the girls and boys came out of the village school the snow was several inches (centimetres) deep, and it was easy to scoop it up in two hands, pat it and shape it into a ball and then throw it at someone else. That was fun even though it was dark.

Oh, yes! I also remember that I was given a clasp knife as a present and that this led to an injury at some time during the Christmas holiday – the second of two unpleasant injuries! I describe this episode in my next memory.

20 A Christmas tree
This gives an impression of some of the traditional ornaments,
including candles which can be very dangerous!

16 Two unpleasant injuries

My mother came down to Somerset on 22nd December 1944, but she was met with an unwelcome surprise!

On the day before she arrived I had fallen over while running along in front of Auntie Margaret, had landed on my face and had broken my front right-hand tooth. It had snapped in half so that the bottom part of the tooth was missing.

Naturally it hurt at the time, because I must have cut my lip as well. I expect that I looked awful. I can still remember that I was on the left of the lane opposite Riverside and running towards Church Street which would take us left towards the cottage.

That was not the only mishap however. One of my Christmas presents was a clasp knife, which had a strong spring so that it was not easy to open and shut it.

It wasn't long before I managed to shut the blade onto my left-hand index finger just on the first joint from my fingernail. Of course it was very painful and I screamed with pain. It bled freely, but fortunately my Auntie Rose was also present and she bandaged my finger for me.

My mother stayed for a week and towards the end of that time it was decided that the bandage should be taken off. Unfortunately it had stuck to the blood and was not easy to remove. I wouldn't let my mother handle it, because it was painful and I felt that she would be too squeamish and therefore too slow.

When I asked Auntie Rose to take it off she didn't waste any time but ripped it off quickly. Although it hurt me again, the pain soon went and my finger continued to heal well. I can still see the faint one-centimetre scar over sixty years later!

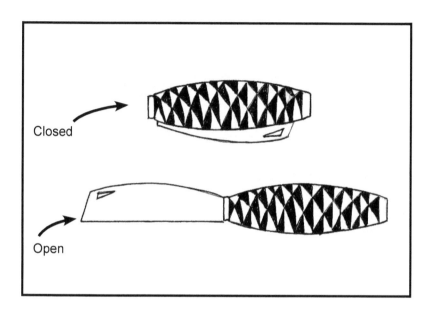

Closed

Open

21 A clasp knife
This gives an impression of my 1944 Christmas present, but I haven't
shown the ring at the end of the handle, by which the knife could be
attached to a belt.

17 Dinder Church

Although Auntie Margaret looked after me during my stay in Somerset, my Auntie Rose was also present for part of the time. When I was baptised and christened in 1936 she was chosen to be my godmother. This means that she had the duty to be responsible for my education in the Christian faith.

The Randalls were a religious family and so I was expected to go to church every week while I was in Dinder. The three daughters were particularly religious and this was probably due to the expectations made of them.

I still have a book, on a shelf in my study, which is entitled 'The Girl's Little Book.' On the front endpaper is the name May Randall and the date February 10th 1896. She must have been fourteen years old when it was given to her. Its sixty pages might well annoy many modern women, because it expects girls to be pure, devout and demure.

It was the custom for us to go to the church service on Sunday morning and then again to Evensong, which took place at about 6.30pm. On several occasions I was asked to pump air for the organ which accompanied the hymns. I held a wooden lever and pumped with my right arm. I had to watch a dial with a needle which showed the air pressure and not let it drop below a certain point. It was very hard work for a little boy of eight and I was glad that it didn't happen very often.

In March 1945 my mother's diary has the entry: "Bernard a choirboy in Dinder." This was an activity which I enjoyed and I probably owe my love of music partly to this experience. A couple of years later, when we were on holiday in Dinder, my mother and I went into Wells and had a photo taken of me in my chorister's uniform – a black cassock and a white surplice. I looked almost angelic!

22 Bernie as a choirboy
This photo was taken when I returned to Somerset for my
summer holiday. Note my missing front tooth!

125

18 Learning prayers

It was probably in the spring of 1945 that one of my aunts encouraged me to take part in a competition in order to win a prayer book. The Book of Common Prayer has been used in Church of England services for several hundred years and it is the custom for each church to provide a hymn book and a prayer book for each member of the congregation.

Some people, however, prefer to take their own prayer book to church and Canon Burnell offered to give a prayer book as the prize for learning prayers over a period of several weeks. He explained to a group of village children that we were required to learn one new prayer each week. This was a special prayer called a 'collect,' each one of which was connected with a particular Sunday, and we were to be tested on it before the church service every Sunday morning.

Needless to say, I forgot all about it during the week until my aunt reminded me about it after breakfast on Sunday. I would then spend half-an-hour doing my best to learn the prayer.

I would leave the cottage, cross the road and go through the lych gate. I would then make my way to the church porch, where the children gathered to be tested. Most of them hadn't bothered to learn the prayer properly and so it happened that eventually I was judged to be the best at reciting the prayers.

Canon Burnell was somewhat slow to produce the prayer book as the prize that I had won and so, when my mother came to see me in April, we walked around to his house on Riverside and my mother persuaded him to hand it over.

I regret to say that I no longer have it, but I'm sure that the mental effort of learning a new text every week was good for me!

23 Dinder church and its lych gate
Many English churches have a lych gate. It has a
roof above it and it was once the custom to leave the
coffin here for a short time before a funeral.

19 My return home

My mother made a note in her diary on Thursday 26th April 1945 that the Prime Minister, Winston Churchill, had announced that the German rocket attacks had come to an end. She wasted no time. She came down to Somerset on Saturday 5th May, I said my goodbyes and we returned to Whetstone on Monday 7th. My life as an evacuated child had come to an end.

My return was sudden and unexpected, but that was a good thing, because it meant that I didn't have time to worry about changing back from one life style to another. Indeed, the timing was just right, because it meant that I was able to finish the spring term in Dinder and start the summer term at a school in Whetstone, having been away for only two terms of primary education.

Those two terms in Dinder were very valuable because they gave me an experience of village life; I also had to adapt to new relationships and changing circumstances. My return marked the end of one formative period of my life and the start of the next.

On Tuesday 8th May 1945, the day after my return to Whetstone, England celebrated VE Day (Victory in Europe Day). Mr. Miles, who lived at the end of our balcony, organised a bonfire and firework party on the grassy patch next to the air-raid shelters.

Unfortunately, soon after the first fireworks had been lit, one of them landed in the box holding the rockets, Jumping Crackers, Roman Candles, Catherine Wheels and other fireworks.

For five minutes the pyrotechnics which resulted were random and unexpected. My mother was frightened that they would break our windows, but they provided a glorious and in some ways fitting ending to my wartime experiences!

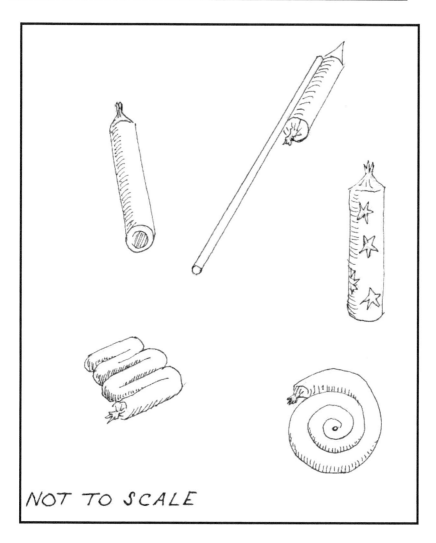

NOT TO SCALE

24 Some popular fireworks
Clockwise from the top left you can see a Banger (a type which
explodes with a loud bang when ignited, hence its name), a Rocket, a
Roman Candle, a Catherine Wheel and a Jumping Cracker.

20 Two holidays at Dinder

Although I left Dinder in 1945, my connection with the Randall family home continued for a further ten years until 1955. Since I had been away from my parents for nine months, it was deemed safe and suitable for me to spend my summer holiday with my aunt. My mother took me down to Somerset on 7th August 1945, stayed until 11th and then left me there for the rest of the month.

It was probably on this occasion that I again met the boy who lived in the last house on the way to Croscombe. I remember him greeting me with the words "Allo, spiv, ow be ee gettn arn?" ("Hello, Spiv, how are you getting on?") During the war there had been some people who made money on the 'Black Market' (i.e. by illegal trading) and they were known as 'spivs' in London. Naturally he associated me with London and therefore called me a spiv.

I have no other memory of that holiday and indeed some of my memories of events in Somerset may have come either from my nine months' evacuation there or from one or two of my later holidays there.

In August 1946 my mother took me to Dinder for two weeks. By that time my Auntie Margaret was very ill and I remember my mother and I pushing her in a wheel chair along the main road to Dulcote and then across the flat fields to Wells.

It was either during this holiday or in the August of the following year that I went to a fête held at the Somerville mansion just beyond the church.

I went in for a *Guess the Weight* competition and was joint winner with a young man who had been a Japanese POW (Prisoner of War). He very kindly said that I didn't need to share it with him and so, having guessed accurately the weight of a box full of luxury foods such as butter, I was able to take it back to the cottage and share it with my mother and aunt.

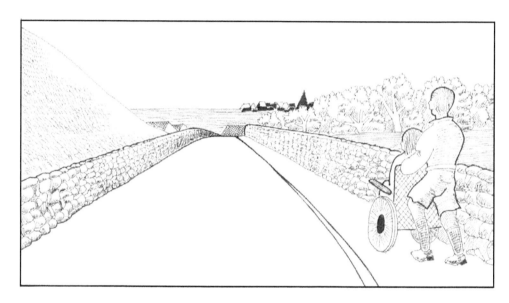

25 Pushing Auntie Margaret in her wheel chair to Wells

21 To the seaside

About twenty miles (thirty kilometres) to the west of Wells is the seaside resort of Burnham-on-Sea, which is famous for its long, flat, sandy beaches. I know that I visited it several times after returning to London, but I believe that I also visited it at least once during my sojourn in Dinder.

I can remember sitting in a bus for what seemed a long time in order to get from Wells to Burnham, but my memory of visiting the beach is clearer still. As the tide ebbed it uncovered a huge expanse of firm sand.

It was possible to ride donkeys along the beach or to sit in a  carriage pulled by horses. Some children had to be lifted onto the donkey and also be steadied by the careful hand of an adult. It was easier, but less exciting, to climb up into a carriage. After the person in charge had been paid, the carriage, or the string of donkeys, would make its way along the beach to a specific place and then turn around and return to the starting point. For a young child it was like being part of an exploration trip!

26 Donkeys on the beach
How many donkeys are there?

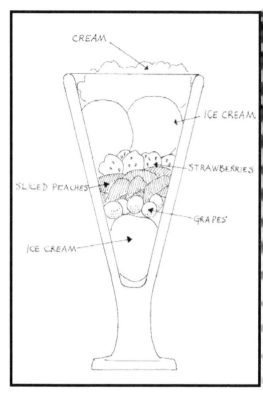

27 A Knickerbocker Glory
This diagrammatic cross-section
shows the various kinds of fruit and
ice cream.

I also remember enjoying the occasional ice cream and on more than one occasion my mother and I had the pleasure of consuming a *Knickerbocker Glory*. This consisted of a mixture of ice cream and fruit (such as strawberries and peaches), which were served in a tall glass so that we had to work our way down through layers of ice cream and fruit until we reached the bottom. Of course, I also enjoyed the fresh air and exercise which came from being at the seaside.

Another reason for visiting Burnham was that Uncle Henry and his wife and daughter lived there. I don't know what his work was, but I have the feeling that, at that time, he and Auntie Nellie may have run a guest house not far from the seafront.

22 Caves and conjuring

The Mendips consist of limestone hills and their geology favours the creation of caves. Wells lies at the southern foot of the Mendip Hills and only a mile to its northwest can be found the Wookey Hole Caves. I can remember visiting these caves, as well as the more famous Cheddar Caves (which are also in the Mendips), but I'm not sure whether or not I went to Wookey during my time as an evacuee. I probably did so during one of my summer holiday visits to Dinder.

Like most people I found the stalactites, stalagmites and other rock formations very impressive. I later discovered my own way to remember the differences in meaning: the sixth letter of *stalaCtite* is '*c*' for ceiling and the sixth letter of *stalaGmite*' is '*g*' for ground. As a stalagmite grew upwards it sometimes joined with a stalactite and thus created a column. In some places they were very beautiful, in others – strange and forbidding.

If one could ignore the other visitors, the whole cave was silent and eerie. Indeed, one rock formation was known as *The Old Woman of Wookey* or alternatively *The Witch of Wookey* which helped to make the caves sound more mysterious than they already were. A small boy could easily believe that the caves were magic places.

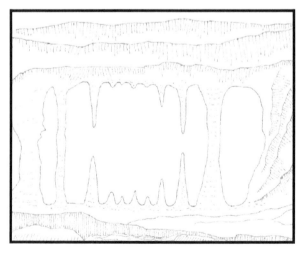

28 Some stalagmites and stalactites
The stalactites hang down.

29 A top hat and magic wand

Mention of witches and magic reminds me that on one occasion I was taken to a village fete somewhere in the area. It was here that I met my first magician – or should I say conjuror? Of course he had a magic wand and I seem to remember that he had a black top hat from which he produced a string of flags and other objects. He performed card tricks and other conjuring tricks and I was very pleased to be one of the children who were invited onto the stage to help him. I went up onto the platform, but I can't remember now what kind of trick he performed or what I had to do.

23 The end of the Randalls in Dinder

It is easy to see, reading between the lines, that I look back at my time in Dinder with nostalgia. Despite the wartime conditions it was a golden period for me, but all good things must come to an end, and my close connections with Somerset became weaker after Auntie Margaret died of her illness on 25th February 1947.

My mother took me to Bristol with Auntie May in order to meet Auntie Rose. Margaret's funeral took place on Saturday 1st March, presumably at Dinder Church, but I couldn't bring myself to look at her in her coffin, because I was frightened of what I might see, never having seen a dead body before. It was enough to have the memory of her as she had been.

Auntie May visited us at Whetstone that summer and then on 29th July took me back with her to Dinder, where I stayed until 2nd September. That was almost the end of my connection with Dinder, because I spent my 1948 and 1949 holidays at Pitsea.

I did return briefly a few more times. In August 1950 my parents and I stayed at the cottage for three days and then returned two weeks later in order to attend the wedding of Joan Randall and William Warner at Burnham.

The next year we went to Swanage for our summer holiday and while there made an excursion to Dinder on Tuesday 7th August. It was fortunate that we were able to see Auntie May on that occasion, because she died three years later in 1954. My mother told me that she had always been fond of her and that they had gone to the theatre together several times before my mother got married.

My final visit to the cottage was in April 1955, when I was preparing for my A-levels (Advanced Level Examinations). We were there for only three nights. My parents returned in July 1956 by which time I was in the army. That was their final visit (thirty-one years after their first visit together), because Auntie Rose went back into service with Mrs. Gilroy and the cottage was eventually sold.

30 Visiting Auntie May in 1951
Here she is with Bernard standing at the gate of the cottage in Dinder.

137

24 The Somervilles in Dinder

I imagine that the Somerville family resided in their Dinder mansion for far longer than the Randalls lived in their humble cottage and yet they left Dinder only a few decades after my maternal relatives. The name Somerville sounds French and therefore suggests that one of their ancestors may have come over with William the Conqueror. It is also possible that most of the land around Dinder belonged to this family and that the local inhabitants were tenant farmers and their employees.

While I was an infant, Sir James Somerville was a vice admiral who became famous for two naval successes. On 3rd July 1940 he sank the French fleet at Oran in North Africa in order to prevent it falling into German hands, and on 27th November of the same year he achieved a spectacular success against the Italian navy on the seas off Sardinia.

When, as young boy, I met him, he seemed very pleasant and took some of us upstairs to the top of the building where there was a toy train-set spread out on a large, bare, wooden floor. I can't help wondering whether or not he was the one who played with it!* He also signed the first page of my new autograph book: "James F. Somerville 20/8/47."

Almost sixty years later in August 2004 my wife and I stayed at Wells overnight on our way back from visiting friends in Exmouth, Devon. The next morning we drove into Dinder, where we met the woman who had bought Church View. She told us that the Somervilles had left Dinder and that the mansion had later been occupied by members of the family which makes the well-known brand of shoes – Clarks Shoes. It seems that not only peasants but also landowners may feel the need to leave their ancestral home!

31 The Somerville mansion
This was the kind of view which I had when I visited the Dinder fête in
August 1947.

25 The Meadows and the Randalls now

George and Mary Randall had three daughters who never married, perhaps because so many men were killed in the trenches of the First World War. Of their three sons, Cyril had a daughter, my mother, and later a son, David, who died unmarried and childless in 2001. Henry had just one child, a daughter, but Edward produced a son and a daughter in South Africa. Unless his son Roy also had a son, Roy must have been the last male descendant of George Randall bearing the name of Randall.

32 The Randalls in South Africa

This photo was taken in December 1944 and shows Uncle Eddie with his wife, Kate, and two children, Joyce and Roy.

33 The Meadows in England
This photo was taken in August 2011 and shows Bernard on the left with John and Anne together with Bernard's wife, Pat, and their younger son, Alex on the right.

However, there are still descendants of Joseph Meadows who bear the Meadows name, because until recently there were still some male descendants living in New Zealand. His eldest son, Charles, had one child, me, and my two children were boys, but whether or not they will have boys of their own remains to be seen. They may be the last male descendants of Joseph Meadows in England. My elder son, John, married Anne Clayton in August 2011 and so time will tell...

Now that I have turned my mind towards family matters it seems strange to me that we mark the progression of the generations by naming children after their fathers. As the old saying goes: *It's a wise child that knows its own father.*

Despite the occasional accidental switching of babies' name tags in hospitals, it's usually clear as to who is the mother of a particular baby. It's the mother who carries the baby as a parasite for several months and then suffers the pain of giving birth to it. She is then the one who bears the brunt of looking after it. How unfair that it isn't given her surname!

According to Julius Caesar in the 1st century BC it was the custom for British women to have more than one husband, but whoever was the husband at the time a baby was born was considered to be the father. Why didn't they count it as the woman's child and leave it at that? Think about it!

26 Four generations (1856-1945)

My great-grandmother, Mary Oatley, was born in 1856, her son, Cyril Randall, was born in 1884, Esme Randall arrived in 1908 and I was born in 1936.

Mary died in 1945, aged 84. In her lifetime the British Isles probably changed more rapidly than at any time before.

When I went to live in the Somerset cottage in 1944, my great-grandmother was still alive and I was in contact with a countryside way of life which, in some ways, was similar to that of the 1880s. When I returned to London in 1945 it was evident that our English way of life could never be the same again. In the second half of the nineteenth century London had been the capital of a worldwide empire greater than any the world had ever seen. For two centuries our small country exploited resources from around the world.

But, in 1945, the country was exhausted; the cost of the war had been considerable - in money, in human suffering and in its effects on the Empire. The people of the colonies continued to demand their independence and within a few post-war years the British Empire had ceased to exist.

My birthplace was the capital of a rich country, but after the war my homeland reverted to being a set of small and relatively insignificant islands. Unfortunately the government and the people have been slow and unwilling to recognise this point of view.

Even while I was at school in the 1950s I decided that we were grossly overcrowded and that we were living on borrowed time. Some people may say that I am guilty of being a Little Englander but, on the contrary, I am proud of my country.

We have produced many first rate creators, inventors and innovators in various fields but have often been handicapped by poor management. Now at the beginning of the 21ˢᵗ century the bubble has burst. We are in a bad way! The question is: do we have the will to recover?

35 Uncle Eddie in South Africa
This 1925 photo shows Uncle Eddie (centre) playing a harmonium in the *Royal Train Jazz Band*. One banjo player was a police inspector, the other was a Chief Electrician, and Eddie was the personal assistant of the Prince of Wales.

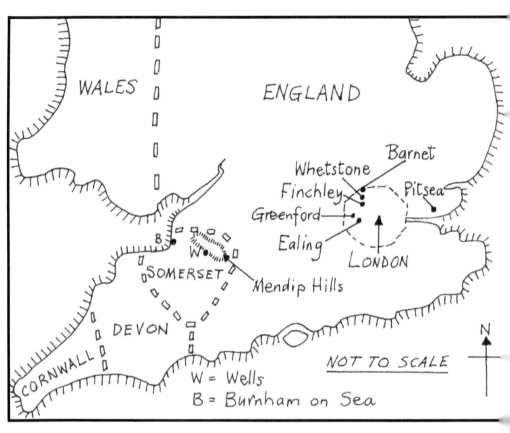

A sketch map of Southern England
This shows the locations of some of the places mentioned in this book. Dinder is close to Wells, itself identified by the letter W.

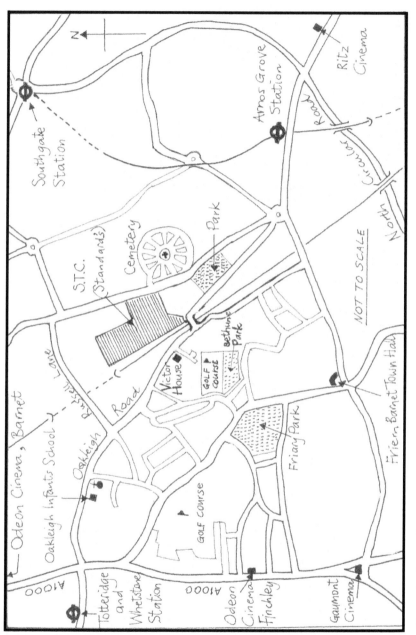

Map of a Part of North London
This map shows some of the places referred to in the text. It is not drawn accurately to scale but covers a region about 3 miles across.

Notes

Notes referred to with asterisks in text

Chapter 1

Memory 8...and in Singing from the Modulator.

This may have meant that she was able to modulate (i.e. change) from one key/scale to another, which is an important part of European music.

Memory 9   37, Walbrook, London, E.C.4

Nowadays the London and national postal districts have a 'Zip code' at the end of each address and there are no full stops between the capital letters, e.g. EC3, EC4, W9, EN5 (London); IP19 (Suffolk), BL9 (Lancashire).

Chapter 2

Memory 10...they only occurred a few times in a year.

This is the usual way in which people would speak and write such a sentence. However, a more accurate (and pedantic) word-order would be: ."...they occurred only a few times in a year."

Memory 16 ...my copy of Giant-Land...

Nowadays this title would not include a hyphen, but my copy has a hyphen because the original book dates back to the late nineteenth or early twentieth century.

Memory 23"There's one born every minute."

This is one way of calling someone 'stupid.' The idea is that every minute of the day someone foolish is born somewhere or other.

Memory 30 These were the last straws!

An Arab story tells of a camel whose owner kept putting straw onto its back. Finally he put one more piece of straw onto the load and this broke the camel's back. The idea is that, after a great many problems, one final little problem may make someone become impatient and/or angry.

Chapter 3

Memory 2...a couple of steps brought one to the porch...

One' is traditional Standard English, meaning 'people in general,' but it is rarely used today. Most people use 'you' to mean the same thing. E.g. "...a couple of steps brought you to the porch...", or "You can fly from London to Hong Kong in about eleven hours."

Memory 6...about the same age as me.

Good Standard English = "the same as I (was). However, 'me' is also good modern English. Most people say "the same as me."

Memory 7...copies of the Daily Mirror...

In 1944 the Daily Mirror was a popular left-wing newspaper which was not as 'heavy' to read as The Times and the Guardian. The Sunday Mirror was published on Sundays. My mother had a copy delivered to our flat every day, but I never saw my father read a newspaper.

Memory 7...strip cartoons...

Each strip consisted of a row of about five or six little pictures which told part of a story, and each story could last for several weeks.

Many of the cartoons contained one or two 'speech bubbles' *or* 'speech balloons' which showed what the characters were saying. They were similar to the strips in children's 'comics' but were in black and white, whereas children's comics sometimes had strip cartoons in colour.

Memory 24 I can't help wondering *whether* or not he was the one who played with it.

Most people now say: "I can't help wondering *if* he was the one who played with it."

Glossary

GLOSSARY

CHAPTER 1

Memory 1

to baptise (verb, Greek-Latin) to drop water onto a baby's head in church in order to show that it is now a Christian

to derive (verb, Latin-French) to get *or* obtain one thing from another

maiden name (noun, Old English) the family name of a girl *or* woman before she is married

twenties, thirties (nouns, English) the years 1920-1929 and 1930-1939

tropical (adj., Greek-Latin) to do with the tropics, i.e. the hot regions on either side of the equator

to dredge (verb, Old English?) to remove sand etc. from a riverbed

to be involved in (verb, Latin) to take part in an activity

operation (noun, Latin) a kind of work *or* activity

Memory 2

ancestor (noun, Latin) a forefather, someone from whom other people are descended

to develop (verb, French) when something changes from one thing into another

to graze (verb, Old English) to eat grass and other plants

to introduce into (verb, Latin) to bring into

surname (noun, French) a family name (originally = a nickname)

current (adj., French) common, widespread

the Norman Conquest In 1066 Duke William of Normandy came to England with an army, killed King Harold, and became the first Norman king of England.

Memory 3

paternal (adj., Latin) to do with the father's side of a family

lay preacher (noun, French) a person who is not a priest but teaches other people about God

occupation (noun, French) work, job

apparently (adv., Latin) it seems that...

chauffeur (noun, French) someone who drives a car for another person

lorry, lorries (noun, C19: Dialect?) a large motor vehicle which can carry heavy loads

van (noun, from **caravan?** Persian-Italian) a motor vehicle which can carry goods from one place to another

Co-operative Society (Latin, French) a firm which sells food and is run for the benefit of the customers

epidemic (noun, Greek-Latin-French) a disease which becomes widespread

Memory 4

maternal (adj., Latin) to do with the mother's side of a family

maiden name (noun, Old English) the family name of an unmarried girl or woman

presumably (adv., Latin-French) one believes that, it is probable that...

financial (adj., French) to do with using/handling money

mansion (noun, Latin-French) a large house belonging to a rich family

groom (noun, Old English) someone who takes care of horses

conductor (noun, Latin) someone who sells *or* checks tickets on a bus *or* tram

mechanised (adj., Latin) to do with machines *or* machinery

eventually (adv., Latin) after some time, finally

rural (adj., Latin-French) to do with the countryside

Memory 5

cottage (noun, Old English) a small house, often in the countryside

bookish (adj., Old English) to do with someone who likes reading books

The Pickwick Papers (1837)   This was a famous novel by Charles Dickens (1812-1870).

apparently (adv., Latin) it seems that…

local (adj., Latin) to do with one particular place

grammar schools (noun phrase, Greek-Latin) schools which were first started in the 16th century so that pupils could study Greek and Latin; they became schools for academic pupils

academic   (adj., Greek-Latin) to do with studying and thinking clearly

digestive (adj., French) to do with eating food so that it changes and becomes part of a body

to undertake (verb, Old English, Norse) to do

doubtless   (adv., Latin-French) probably *or* without doubt, certainly

initial (noun, Latin) the first letter of a word

teens (noun) the years of life between the ages of 13 and 19

Memory 6

eventually (adv., Latin) after some time, finally

sound-recording engineer (noun phrase, Latin-French) someone who helps to record people playing music *or* speaking

reference (noun, Latin) a letter which tells other people about how good or bad someone is

manager (noun, Latin-Italian) someone who runs a firm *or* part of a firm

to concern (verb, Latin) to be of interest to someone

to employ (verb, Latin-French) to give work to someone

company (noun, Latin-French) a firm

conscientious (adj., Latin) careful and hardworking

capable (adj., Latin) able to do something well

initiative (noun, Latin) the ability to think of new ideas

factory (noun, Latin) a large building where people make things

advisory capacity (noun phrase, Latin) a job where someone gives advice *or* tells other people what to do

to dispense with his services (phrase, Latin-French) to stop employing him, to stop giving him work

without reservations (phrase, Latin-French) certainly, without any doubt

Memory 7

colloquial (adj., LATIN) to do with the common, everyday language which people speak

to prefer (verb, Latin) to like one thing better than another

privilege (noun, Latin-French) a special right to be allowed to do something

equivalent (adj., Latin) of similar or equal value; when two or more things are the same

armed forces (noun phrase, Latin, Latin-French) the army, navy and air-force; soldiers of one kind or another

squint (noun, Dutch?) when a person has one eye not looking in the same direction as the other

to exempt (verb, Latin) to excuse someone from doing something

outbreak (noun, Old English) the sudden start of something, e.g. disease, war

Memory 8

rheumatism (noun, Greek-Latin) an illness which causes pain in joints and muscles

ailment (noun, Old English) illness

capable (adj., Latin) able to do well

to develop (verb, French) to cause something to change, grow *or* get better

certificate (noun, Latin-French) a paper *or* document which says that something is true

to certify (verb, Latin-French) to say that something is true, usually in writing

to indicate (verb, Latin) to show

choir (noun, Latin-French) a group of people who sing songs

branch (noun, Latin-French) part of a larger group *or* thing

elementary (adj., Latin) to do with the first steps of an activity

London County Council At one time this was the local government for London.

prescribe (verb, Latin) to command, to lay down as a rule *or* an order

Memory 9

reference (noun, Latin) a letter which tells other people about how good or bad someone is

employer (noun, Latin-French) someone who gives work to other people

druggist (noun, French) a shop *or* firm which provides medicines

sundries (noun, Old English) different kinds of things

wholesale (noun, Old English) the selling of goods to shops in large quantities

to export (verb, Latin) to send goods out of one country and into another

to concern (verb, Latin) to be important *or* of interest to someone

to certify (verb, Latin-French) to say that something is true, usually in writing

in my employment (adverbial phrase) working for me

depression of business (noun phrase) fewer markets, less trade, less work for the people in his firm

entire (adj., Latin-French) whole, complete

indicated (past participle, Latin) shown, suggested

Memory 10

emotional (adj., Latin-French) to do with one's feelings *or* emotions e.g. being happy, sad, angry

darling (adj., Old English) dear, (someone who is) loved

to vex (verb, Latin-French) to annoy, to make angry

Xmas (noun, Greek-Latin) Christmas, a Christian festival which always takes place on 25th December

to bless (verb, Old English) to wish someone well, to protect someone from harm

to enclose (verb, French-Latin) to put one thing inside another

heart-breaking (adj., Old English) making someone sad *or* unhappy

guilty (adj., Old English) to do with thinking *or* feeling that you have done something wrong *or* bad

Memory 11

suffered from depression (phrase) felt very unhappy

to occur (verb, Latin) to happen, to take place, to come about

Accounts Department (noun, French) the part of a firm where people keep records of how other people handle the money

Picture Corporation (noun, Latin) a film company

on the way to recovery (phrase) getting better, becoming less ill

services (noun, Latin-French) work, the help that someone gives

omission (noun, Latin) something not done

pressure of work (phrase) being very busy

bout (noun, German?) a period of time when one is ill

be that as it may (phrase) however

acute (adj., Latin) severe, extreme

Memory 12

ancestor (noun, Latin) a forefather, someone from whom other people are descended

sibling (noun, Old English) a brother or sister

to assume (verb, Latin) to believe, to suppose

paternal (adj. Latin) to do with the father's side of a family

to inherit (verb, Latin-French) to receive something from someone who has died

bible (noun, Greek-Latin-French) the holy book of Christians

presumably (adv., Latin-French) one believes that, it is probable that

birth certificate (noun, Norse, Latin-French) an official document which gives information about a child and its parents when it is born

cathedral (noun, Latin) a very large church, the 'seat' of a bishop

to baptise (verb, Greek-Latin) to drop water onto a baby's head in church in order to show that it is now a Christian

labourer (noun, Latin-French) a worker who does not need much skill

maiden name (noun, Old English) the family name of a girl *or* woman before she is married

Memory 13

sibling (noun, Old English) a brother or sister

great-uncle (noun, Old English) an uncle of one's father *or* mother

great-aunt (noun, Old English) an aunt of one's father *or* mother

Memory 14

cottage (noun, Old English) a small, simple house, usually in the countryside

obvious (adj., Latin) clear, easy to see *or* understand

pilgrim (noun, Latin) someone who makes a special journey to a holy place

cathedral (noun, Latin) a very large church, the 'seat' of a bishop

mains water (noun, Old English) the water which goes to houses and other buildings along pipes

privy (noun, Latin-French) a small toilet, often in an outhouse *or* shed

chamber (noun, Latin-French) a room

illumination (noun, Latin) light, lighting

to undertake (verb, Old English, Norse) to do

undertaken done

stove (noun, Old English) a heater *or* cooker which burns wood *or* coal

battery (noun, Latin-French) a group of cells which produces electricity

to exchange (verb, Latin) to give one thing and receive something else in return

Memory 15

to be impressed by (verb, Latin) to be influenced by

to assume (verb, Latin) to believe, to suppose

hobby (noun, 14th cent. English) a pastime, something which one does in one's spare time for pleasure

to entitle (verb, Latin-French) to give a name *or* title to something

shot (noun, Old English) a picture *or* scene in a film; a length of film without a break

sub-title (noun, Latin) a title, name *or* word which is not as important as the main title

typical (adj., Greek-Latin) to do with something which is usual *or* is a normal example

brief (adj., Latin-French) short

familiarity (noun, Latin) when something is well-known

CHAPTER 2

Memory 1

maternity hospital (noun, Latin) a hospital in which women are helped to give birth to babies

mongrel (noun, Old English) an animal which comes from a mixture of breeds *or* races

definition (noun, Latin) when one gives the meaning of a word *or* phrase

various (adj., Latin) of different kinds, not all the same

to intermarry (verb, Latin, French) when people from different cultures *or* groups get married

descendant (noun, Latin-French) someone who descends from someone else, i.e. children descend from their parents, grandparents etc.

to invade (verb, Latin) to enter and attack someone else's land

population (noun, Latin) the people who live in one particular place *or* country

to conscript (verb, Latin) to force people to join an army, navy *or* air force

indigenous (adj., Latin) to do with native people, those people living in the place where they were born

to establish themselves (verb, Latin-French) to settle down and stay in a place

Vikings (name, Norse) the men who left Norway, Denmark and Sweden, who first attacked other European countries and then settled in them

eventually (adv., Latin) after some time, finally

to occur (verb, Latin) to happen, to take place, to come about

aristocracy (noun, Greek-Latin) people who are in the top level *or* class in a country, are often big landowners and are usually the rulers

Memory 2

slight (adj., Norse) a little, not much, a small amount

toddler (noun, unknown) a young child who finds it difficult to walk

shot (noun, Old English) a piece of film without a break; a picture *or* scene in a film

perambulator, pram (noun, Latin) a small carriage for babies

sequence (noun, Latin) a series; a group of things which come one after the other

hide-and-seek (noun, Old English) a children's game in which one of them looks for *or* tries to find the others who are hiding

curly (adj., Dutch) curved, not straight

wavy (adj., Old English) looking like waves

drama (noun, Greek-Latin) like a play in a theatre, having emotional interest

to crouch (verb, French) to squat, to bend the legs so that one's body is close to the ground

process (noun, Latin-French) a series of actions, the way of doing something

deck (noun, Dutch) one of the floors on a ship

deck chair (noun) a folding chair made of wood and cloth for use in the open air

occasionally (adv., Latin) not often, from time to time

to clamber (verb, Old English) to climb with difficulty

Memory 3

personal (adj., Latin-French) to do with one particular person

semidetached (adj., Latin, French) to do with a one family house which is joined to another, similar house

presumably (adv., Latin-French) one believes that, it is probable that

flat (noun, Old English) an apartment; a dwelling in a large building in which all the rooms are on the same floor

to occupy (verb, Latin-French) to take up space in something; to live in a house etc.

to occur (verb, Latin) to happen, to take place, to come about

parlour (noun, French) a special room *or* shop

façade (noun, Italian-French) the front of a building

counter (noun, Latin-French) a kind of table in a shop *or* café which is used to serve customers

cornet (noun, Latin-French) a kind of thin biscuit shaped like a cone which is used for holding ice cream

to melt (verb, Old English) to change from a solid to a liquid, just as ice can change to water

Mickey = Michael (name) an important angel in the Bible

mouse (noun, Greek-Latin-Old English) a very small mammal with big ears and a long tail

Mickey Mouse (name) a talking mouse who looked like a human being in some of the cartoons of the American film-maker Walt Disney

costume (noun, Italian-French) a set of special clothes

cartoon (noun, Italian) a funny *or* humorous picture; a film made by taking photos of many drawings

to scream (verb, German) to shout out with pain, fear *or* anger

fright (noun, Old English) a sudden fear

Memory 4

distinct (adj., Latin) clear, easy to see

to occur (verb, Latin) to happen, to take place, to come about

to retrain (verb, French-Latin) to study again in order to work better

to enable (verb, Latin) to make something possible

civil (adj., Latin-French) to do with the people *or* citizens of a country

service (noun, Latin-French) help, assistance

the Civil Service (name) the people who help the government to run a country

aeronautical (adj., Greek) to do with aeroplanes (planes, aircraft)

inspection (noun, Latin) the act of inspecting *or* looking at something

department (noun, French) a part *or* section of a shop, business *or* other organisation

radar (noun, Latin-French) equipment used for detecting moving objects such as aircraft *or* ships

cable (noun, Latin-French) a bundle of wires (like a thick rope) which can conduct electricity (i.e. take electricity from one place to another)

flat (noun, Old English) an apartment; a dwelling in a large building in which all the rooms are on the same floor

factory (noun, Latin) a large building where people make things

commercial (adj., Latin) to do with trade *or* business

estate (noun, Latin-French) an area of houses, factories *or* businesses

site (noun, Latin) the piece of land where something is situated *or* located

particular (adj., Latin-French) to do with a single thing

double-decker (noun, Latin-French, Dutch) a bus with two decks/floors one above the other

sooty (adj., Old English) black like soot (the powder left after a fire)

Memory 5

block of flats (noun phrase, Dutch, Old English) a large building with a number of flats *or* apartments in it

spectacles (noun, Latin-French) (eye)glasses, a pair of lenses for someone who cannot see very well

occasion (noun, Latin) one period of time when something happens

to wrestle (verb, Old English) to fight someone by holding and throwing him or her to the ground

playground (noun, Old English) a place where children can play in the open air

to mend (verb, Latin-French) to repair something which is broken *or* is not working properly

pantry (noun, Latin-French) a small room in which people keep food and kitchen equipment

balcony (noun, Italian) a platform *or* walkway on the outside wall of a building

garage (noun, French) a building in which to store cars *or* other vehicles

parallel (adj., Greek) when two lines keep *or* remain the same distance apart however long they are

Memory 6

parallel (adj., Greek) when two lines keep *or* remain the same distance apart however long they are

roughly (adv., Old English) approximately, not exactly

marble (adj., Greek-Latin) made of a hard rock which is often used for making statues *and* buildings

counter (noun, Latin-French) a kind of table in a shop *or* café which is used to serve customers

to queue (verb, Latin-French) to stand in a line while waiting for something

service road (noun, Latin-French, Old English) a side road in front of a row of shops, houses, offices, businesses *or* factories

parade (noun, Latin-French) a row of shops along a road *or* street

storey (noun, Latin) a floor *or* level of a house *or* other building

to lack (verb, Dutch?) to be without something which one needs

height (noun, Old English) the distance from the bottom of something to its top

length (noun, Old English) the distance from the beginning of something to its end

Confectioner's (shop) (noun, Latin-French) a shop selling chocolate and other sweets

Tobacconist's (shop) (noun, Spanish) a shop selling cigarettes, cigars and tobacco

greengrocer's (shop) (noun, Old English, French) a shop selling fruit and vegetables

grocer's (shop) (noun, French) a shop which sells different kinds of food

hardware shop (noun, Old English) a shop which sells metal goods, e.g. kitchen equipment, other things for the home and tools for the house and the garden

barber's (shop) (noun, Latin-French) a shop where someone cuts men's hair *and* may shave them or trim their beards

combined (adj., Latin) joined together; when one thing can be used in two ways

Memory 7

to consist of (verb, Latin) to be made of

junction (noun, Latin) where two things join together

crossbar (noun, Latin, French) a bar or line which is placed above something else

eventually (adv., Latin) after some time, finally

combined (adj., Latin) joined together; when one thing can be used in two ways

balcony (noun, Italian) a platform *or* walkway on the outside wall of a building

bunker (noun, Scottish) something which is used to store things

latch (noun, Old English) a small bar which is used to keep a door shut

plank (noun, Latin-French) a long piece of flat wood

supply (noun, Latin-French) a quantity, an amount of something

vertically (adv., Latin) upright

to trudge (verb, unknown) to walk slowly and with difficulty

to position (verb, Latin) to put something in a place carefully

to tip (verb, unknown) to drop something at an angle

to create (verb, Latin) to make something – especially something new

Memory 8

central heating (noun, Greek-Latin, Old English) a way of heating the rooms in a building by using pipes *or* tubes

shovel (noun, Old English) a tool used for lifting *and* moving earth, coal etc.

ash (noun, Old English) the material which is left after something has been burnt

to wrap (verb, unknown) to fold *or* turn paper *or* cloth around something else

dustbin (noun, Old English) a metal container for holding household waste

grate (noun, Latin-French) a framework of metal bars for holding fuel in a fireplace

to crumple (verb, German) to crush *or* push something into itself so that it takes up less space

draught (UK), **draft** (USA) (noun, Norse?) a current *or* stream of air

chimney (noun, Greek-Latin-French) the part of a building which carries smoke away from a fire

to ignite (verb, Latin) to set on fire, to make something burn

alight (adj., Old English) on fire, when something is burning

Memory 9

disadvantage (noun, Latin-French) something which is unhelpful *or* unsuitable

to create (verb, Latin) to make something - especially something new

soot (noun, Old English) the black powder which is found in chimneys after a fire

chimney (noun, Greek-Latin-French) the part of a building which takes smoke away from a fire

vast (adj., Latin) huge, very big

neighbourhood (noun, Old English) the area where a group of people live

flame (noun, Latin-French) the burning gas which comes from a fire

consequently (adv., Latin) as a result, when one thing follows another

to employ (verb, Latin-French) to give work to someone

to sweep (verb, Old English) to clean something with a brush *or* broom

grate (noun, Latin-French) a framework of metal bars for holding fuel in a fireplace

ashes (noun, Old English) the material – usually grey – which is left after something has been burnt

make straight for (verb, Old English) to go directly towards something without turning to left or right

sheet (noun, Old English) a flat piece of cloth which is put onto a bed

to position (verb, Latin) to put something in a place carefully

section (noun, Latin) a piece *or* part of something

brush (noun, French) a tool which is used for cleaning surfaces

disc (noun, Greek-Latin) something which is shaped like a flat dinner plate

mounted (past participle, Latin-French) attached; put *or* placed onto something and then fixed firmly

flexible (adj., Latin) able to bend without breaking

to screw (verb, Latin-French) to turn something around and around so that it goes into something else

Memory 10

disadvantage (noun, Latin-French) something which is unhelpful *or* not suitable

smoke (noun, Old English) the material which rises into the air from a fire

fuel (noun, Latin-French) something which can be burnt in order to give us heat *and/or* light

chimney (noun, Greek-Latin-French) the part of a building which takes smoke away from a fire

fog (noun, unknown) thick mist, a cloud on the ground

dense (adj., Latin) when many things are close together *or* crowded

peasouper (noun, Greek-Latin, French) a fog with a greenish colour which reminds us of pea soup

health (noun, Old English) the welfare *or* condition of our body, how well we are

safety (noun, Latin-French) when one is safe, i.e. there is no danger

lungs (noun, Old English) the two organs in our chest which help us to breathe air

to feature (verb, Latin-French) to be an important part of something

to suffer (verb, Latin-French) to experience pain or something unpleasant

impression (noun, Latin) the understanding which comes from an experience

to occur (verb, Latin) to happen, to take place, to come about

to ensure (verb, French) to make sure *or* certain

smokeless fuel (noun, Old English, Latin-French) fuel which gives off little or no smoke

central heating (noun, Greek-Latin, Old English) a way of heating the rooms in a building by using pipes *or* tubes

pollution (noun, Latin) harmful waste materials on the land *or* in the sea

nature (noun, Latin-French) the original, basic *or* fundamental quality of something

fume (noun, Latin-French) a gas, smoke *or* smell which is poisonous, i.e. bad for us

haze (noun, unknown) when the air is not clear because of mist *or* dust in it

obvious (adj., Latin) clear, easy to see *or* understand

frequent (adj., Latin) when something happens often

Memory 11

virtually (adv., Latin) nearly so, almost true

domestic (adj., Latin-French) to do with the house *or* home

computer (noun, Latin) electronic equipment originally used for problems in arithmetic but now used for sending messages etc.

to undertake (verb, Old English) to do

to encourage (verb, Latin-French) to help someone to feel better about doing something

relatively (adv., Latin) quite, fairly, rather

passive (adj., Latin) inactive, not doing anything, not taking part

infancy (noun, Latin) the time when one is an infant *or* very young child

draughts (noun, Norse) a very old game for two players

to consist of (verb, Latin) to be made of, to be formed of

board (noun, Old English) a flat piece of wood *or* cardboard

Memory 12

to provide (verb, Latin) to give, to make available

patriotic (adj., Latin-French) having love for one's country

morale (noun, French) how good *or* confident someone feels; a good feeling

boost (noun, unknown) help; a push upwards

Hitler, Adolf (1889-1945) a German leader, born in Austria, whose actions in Europe helped to lead to World War II

plot (noun, Old English) the story-line in a book, play, film *or* radio play

catch phrase (noun, Latin-French, Greek-Latin) a saying which is often used by one person and becomes well-known

to assist (verb, Latin-French) to help

sound effect (noun, French, Latin) a man-made sound which helps the listener to believe that something is really happening

to disguise (verb, French) to change the way that something looks

advantage (noun, Latin-French) something which is helpful *or* suitable

to encourage (verb, Latin-French) to help someone to feel better about doing something

imagination (noun, Latin) the ability to have new ideas *or* to think about something that one hasn't experienced

to be aware (verb, Old English) to know

to realise (verb, Latin-French) to know *or* understand suddenly

national (adj., Latin) to do with a country *or* nation

service (noun, Latin-French) help, assistance

National Service the time when all young men had to go into the army, navy *or* air-force, e.g. for two years

Memory 13

valuable (adj., Latin-French) expensive, having great value

biscuit tin (noun, French, Old English) a metal box for keeping biscuits fresh

to construct (verb, Latin) to make, to build

to collapse (verb, Latin) to fall down

to suppose (verb, Latin-French) to think, to believe

permissible (adj., Latin) to be allowed, something may be done

to originate (verb, Latin-French) to start *or* to come from

to hunt (verb, Old English) to chase *or* to look for something

to rescue (verb, Latin-French) to save something from danger

enterprising (adj., Latin-French) willing to try out *or* follow new ideas

to manufacture (verb, Latin) to make things, e.g. in a factory

Memory 14

to ration (verb, Latin-French) to limit, to restrict how much people may have of something

in short supply (phrase, Old English, Latin-French) people could not get very much

to starve (verb, Old English) to be very hungry *or* to die of hunger

occasion (noun, Latin) the time when something happens

corn (noun, Old English) Indian corn, maize

flake (noun, Norse?) a small thin piece of something

cornflakes (trade name) an American breakfast cereal made from maize

cereal (noun, Latin) a plant such as rice, wheat, oat *and* rye

to boil (verb, Latin-French) to heat water so that it moves violently *and* makes bubbles

egg cup (noun, Old English) a small cup for holding a single egg

shell (noun, Old English) the hard outside part of an egg

to peel (verb, Old English) to take off *or* remove the outside of an egg etc.

to sprinkle (verb, Dutch?) to drop little bits of something over another thing

to slice (verb, French) to cut something into thin pieces

yolk (noun, Old English) the orange *or* yellow part of an egg

to dip (verb, Old English) to put something into a liquid and then take it out

slice (noun, French) a thin piece which has been cut from something

rare (adj., Latin) not frequent, not common, seldom found

invariably (adv., Latin) always

topside (noun, Old English) a special cut of beef

to roast (verb, German-French) to put meat, vegetables etc. into an oven *or* cooker

Brussels (noun, Flemish) the capital city of Belgium

sprout (noun, Old English) the new bud of a plant which has many leaves on top of each other

Brussels sprouts (noun) very small cabbages which grow together on a single stem

dessert (noun, French) a sweet course *or* dish at the end of a meal

to mince (verb, Latin-French) to cut something up into very small pieces – often by using a machine

savoury (adj., Latin-French) tasty but not sweet

Memory 15

famous (adj., Latin) well-known by many people

precious (adj., Latin-French) valuable, worth a lot of money

union (noun, Latin) a group of workers who have joined together

to produce (verb, Latin) to make

slogan (noun, Scottish [Gaelic – originally meant 'battle-cry'] a short saying

to contain (verb, Latin-French) to keep *or* to hold things in a limited area

cockpit (noun, Old English) the part of a plane in which the pilot *or* pilots sit

worried (adj., Old English) when someone is anxious *and* cannot relax

avid (adj., Latin) keen, eager *and* wanting to do something special

Memory 16

series (noun, Latin) a group of things which come one after the other

to feature (verb, Latin) to make use of something

dachshund (noun, German) a kind of small dog with a long body and short legs

mayor (noun, Latin-French) the leader of a town government

to grouse (verb, unknown) to complain, to say that one is unhappy about something

to describe (verb, Latin) to write or say what something looks like

fairy (noun, Latin-French) an imaginary spirit

sentimental (adj., Latin) to do with feeling very emotional about something

giant (noun, French) huge, much larger than normal

varied (adj., Latin) of several different kinds, not all the same

to grip (verb, Old English) to hold firmly *or* strongly

gripping (adj., Old English) very interesting, thrilling, able to hold one's attention

to battle (verb, Latin-French) to fight, to struggle

Memory 17

local (adj., Latin-French) to do with one particular place

crossroads (noun, Old English) the place where two roads cross each other

to consist of (verb, Latin) to be made of

single-storied (adj., Latin) having only one floor *or* storey

helmet (noun, French) a kind of hat which protects one's head

tin hat (noun, Old English) the popular name for the steel helmet worn by British soldiers and sailors during the Second World War

Memory 18

to provide (verb, Latin) to give, to make available

gas (noun, Greek) something which is like the air *and* is not a liquid or a solid

mask (noun, Arabic-Italian) something which covers one's face *or* part of the face

gas mask (noun) a special mask which can protect one from poisonous gas

to evacuate (verb, Latin-French) to leave a dangerous place

civilian (noun, Latin) someone who is not in the army, navy *or* air force

to be required (verb, Latin-French) to be told to do something, to be ordered

Mickey Mouse (see Chapter Two Memory 3)

claustrophobic (adj., Latin, Greek) unable to bear being in a small space *or* place

to suffocate (verb, Latin) to be unable to breathe

to panic (verb, Greek-Latin-French) to be very frightened

air raid (noun, Greek-Latin-French, Scottish) an attack by aircraft

warning (noun, Old English) when someone or something tells people that danger is coming

shelter (noun, unknown) a place where one can be safe from danger

slate (noun, French) a kind of blue-grey rock which is often used for making roofs

damp (adj., German) when something has some water in it *or* on it

dismal (adj., Latin) to do with making people feel sad *or* unhappy

Memory 19

light (adj., Old English) bright, with lots of light *or* sunshine

airy (adj., Greek-Latin-French) with plenty of space so that one can breathe easily

to attach (verb, French) to join one thing to another

bench (noun, Old English) a kind of long seat usually made of wood

to file in (verb, Latin-French) when people go somewhere one after the other

horizontal (adj., Greek-Latin) flat, level, in line with the horizon

occasion (noun, Latin) the time when something happens

to copy out (verb, Latin) to look at a text and write down the same words

famous (adj., Latin) well-known by many people

character (noun, Greek-Latin) someone in a book, film *or* play

fiction (noun, Latin) a story which is not true but comes from one's imagination

to steal (stole, stolen) (verb, Old English) to take something which belongs to someone else

at great speed (adv., Old English) very quickly

glade (noun, unknown) an open space in a forest *or* wood

needless to say (adv. phrase) of course, it is true that…

I didn't manage to (phrase) I wasn't able to…

at one stage (phrase) at one time, at a certain period

match stick (noun, French, Old English) a wooden match – used to make fire

to borrow (verb, Old English) to take something from someone else for a short time before giving it back

combination (noun, Latin) a joining together of two things

Memory 20

to the best of my knowledge (phrase) I think that…, so far as I know

deliberate (adj., Latin) on purpose, with intention, intended

to make an attempt (phrase) to try

nevertheless (sentence connector, Old English) however, yet; in spite of that…

tub (noun, Dutch) a small pot *or* container

vivid (adj., Latin) very bright to look at

to produce (verb, Latin) to make

to take for granted (verbal phrase) to believe *or* to assume

drawback (noun, Old English) a disadvantage, something which is unhelpful

unappetising (adj., Latin-French) not tasty, unpleasant to eat

mutton (noun, French) the meat of sheep

to coat (verb, French) to cover all over something

to swallow (verb, Old English) to make food go down one's throat to the stomach

to gag (verb, 15th Cent. English) to feel sick and want to vomit

reflex action (noun, Latin) the immediate response of one's body to a stimulus

routine (noun, French) a habit, i.e. when one does something regularly

bye-bye (sentence substitute, 16ᵗʰ Cent. English: "God be with you.") The way that little children say "Good-bye."

Memory 21

to be affected by (verb, Latin) to be influenced by

ailment (noun, Old English) illness, sickness

to suffer (verb, Latin-French) to experience something bad, e.g. pain

entry (noun, Latin-French) a note, a piece of writing in a notebook *or* diary etc.

to be confined (verb, Latin) to be kept in one place *or* space

delirium (noun, Latin) a feeling of confusion in one's mind *or* brain, rather like a very strange dream, which is caused by illness

perception (noun, Latin) the understanding which comes from our senses, e.g. what we see, feel *and* hear

to distort (verb, Latin) to change the shape of something

eiderdown (noun, Norse) a bed cover which is filled with special duck feathers

conflicting (adj., Latin) opposite, contradictory, in opposition – as if fighting

sensation (noun, Latin) a feeling which comes from our senses, e.g. sight, hearing

optical (adj., Greek-Latin) to do with our eyes

illusion (noun, Latin) a false appearance; when something is not what it seems *or* looks like

optical illusion (noun phrase) a picture where the same image first looks like one thing and then can look like something else, e.g. an old woman *and then* a young woman

dread (noun, Old English) great fear

evil (adj., Old English) very bad, wicked

entity (noun, Latin) a thing *or* being

evil entity (noun phrase) a very bad thing, something nasty

drug (noun, French) something which people swallow *or* take into themselves for pleasure, but which then makes them want to continue taking it

teenager (noun, 20th Cent. English?) someone aged 13 to 19

Memory 22

to be affected by (verb, Latin) to be influenced by

nevertheless (sentence connector, Old English) however, yet; in spite of that

to impinge (verb, Latin) to have an affect

air-raid shelter (see Chapter Two Memory 18)

in a row (phrase, Old English) a group of things in a line

plot (noun, Old English) a small piece of land

brick (noun, French) a block of hard clay used for making houses *and* other buildings

concrete (noun, Latin) a wet material used for making roads *and* buildings, which becomes hard when it is dry

air-raid warning (see Chapter Two Memory 18)

siren (noun, Greek-Latin-French) a piece of equipment which can make a loud noise

local (adj., Latin) to do with one particular place

to wrap (verb, unknown) to fold, wind *or* turn something (e.g. paper, cloth) around something else

smelly (adj., French) having a strong, bad *or* nasty smell

slatted (adj., French) having several narrow, thin strips *or* pieces of wood close together

tier (noun, French) a row, layer *or* level, e.g. a set of seats in a cinema *or* theatre

'all clear' (noun, Old English, Latin-French) the signal which was given after an air raid to tell people that it was safe to leave their shelters

to drag (verb, Old English) to pull something with difficulty

cosy (adj., unknown?) warm *and* comfortable, snug

Memory 23

domestic (adj., Latin-French) to do with the house *or* home

to restrict (verb, Latin) to keep something within limits

episode (noun, Greek) something which happens as part of a series

to indicate (verb, Latin) to show

actual (adj., Latin) true, real

queue (noun, Latin-French) a line of people waiting for something

adult (noun, Latin) a mature, grownup person

to realise (verb, Latin-French) to know *or* understand suddenly

insensitive (adj., Latin) unfeeling, not understanding the feelings of other people

docks (noun, Dutch) an area where ships stop so that people can load and unload their cargoes (i.e. the goods which they carry)

agonisingly (adv., Greek-Latin) very, extremely *or* desperately

facilities (noun, Latin) the equipment which is suitable for a particular purpose

to be relieved (verb, Latin-French) to feel happy, to feel better than one was before

Memory 24

Plasticine (trade name) a kind of clay used for making models

destroyer (noun, Latin-French) a small, fast warship which was used for hunting submarines

realistic (adj., Latin-French) looking like the real thing

laconic (adj., Greek-Latin) using few words, not speaking very much

hint (noun, unknown) a suggestion *or* indication about something

tragedy (noun, Greek-Latin-French) a shocking *or* sad event

trunks (noun, Latin-French) a swimming costume for boys *and* men, rather like underpants

slide (noun, Old English) a smooth, sloping platform which one can slide down

to slide (slid, slid) (verb, Old English) to slip, to move smoothly along a surface

queue (noun, Latin-French) a line of people waiting for something

platform (noun, French) a flat surface on which people can stand

turn (noun, Greek-Latin-French-Old English) the time *or* opportunity to do something

patiently (adv., Latin-French) waiting for some time without becoming angry

to sink (sank, sunk) (verb, Old English) to drop down *or* descend into a liquid such as water

to drown (verb, Old English?) to die in water because one cannot get air to breathe

be that as it may (phrase) however; whatever the truth may be; the facts concerning something are not important

Memory 25

pastime (noun, Latin-French?, Old English?) a hobby, something that one does in one's spare time, i.e. when one is not working

to go to the pictures (phrase) to go the cinema to see a film *or* films

cartoon (noun, Italian) a film made by taking photos of many drawings

sentimental (adj., Latin) when a person feels very emotional about something

dwarf (noun, Old English) a person who is very much smaller than most people

wicked (adj., Old English) evil, morally bad, deliberately doing things which hurt *or* harm other people

stepmother (noun, Old English) a woman who marries one's father after the real mother has died *or* been divorced

combination (noun, Latin) a joining together of two things

wonderful (adj., Old English) splendid, marvellous, extremely fine, excellent

fairy tale (noun, Latin-French, Old English) a story about magical things for young children

folk story (noun, Old English, Latin-French) a traditional story which was originally told by ordinary people but was not written down

comic (adj., Greek-Latin) funny, humorous, something which makes people laugh

joke (noun, Latin) a very short *and* funny story which makes people laugh

audience (noun, Latin-French) the people who listen to the radio; those who watch a play, film, television *or* other show

costume (noun, Italian-French) a suit of clothes like a uniform

stage set (noun, Latin-French, Old English) the scenery for a play *or* other show

Memory 26

teenager (noun) someone between the ages of 13 and 19

National Service (see Chapter Two Memory 12)

merely (adv., Latin) only

to provide (verb, Latin) to give *or* to make available

luxurious (adj., Latin-French) looking very expensive, costing a lot of money

surroundings (noun, Latin-French) the area *or* conditions around a person

to consist of (verb, Latin) to be made of

spacious (adj., Latin-French) having a lot of space *or* area

design (noun, Latin) shape *or* form

sloping (adj., Old English) not level, lying at an angle

magical (adj., Greek- French) being beyond our normal, real, everyday experience

palace (noun, Latin-French) a large and expensive building belonging to a king, queen *or* prince etc.

Memory 27

to bring up (brought, brought) (verb, Old English) to care for *or* look after a child while it is growing up into an adult

strictly (adv., Latin) harshly, severely *or* following rules closely

naughty (adj., 14ᵗʰ Cent. English) behaving badly, badly behaved

to spank (verb, 18ᵗʰ Cent. English) to hit *or* slap with the open and flat hand, usually on the buttocks

to strike (struck, struck) (verb, Old English) to hit

leather (noun, Old English) a strong material made from the skin *or* hide of an animal

punishment (noun, Latin-French) when someone is made to pay *or* suffer for doing something bad *or* wrong

buttocks (noun, 13ᵗʰ Cent. English) the part of the body on which people sit

to be aware (verb, Old English) to know

on the contrary (phrase) not at all, quite the opposite

to discipline (verb, Latin) to help people to behave well *or* to control themselves

the universe (noun, Latin-French) the stars and all the other matter which we can see in space

to consider (verb, Latin) to think about something *or* to believe

ironic (adj., unknown?) seeing the humour in an idea which is inconsistent, illogical *or* a contradiction

violent (adj., Latin) using a great deal of force

gentle (adj., Latin) not using much force; having a mild and kindly nature, personality *or* character

183

Memory 28

to spoil (verb, Latin-French) to give a child everything that it wants

adage (noun, Latin-French) a proverb, a traditional saying

to contradict (verb, Latin) to say the opposite of what someone else says

to compensate (verb, Latin) to provide a balance, "to make up for..."

deficiency (noun, Latin) a shortage *or* a lack of something

chatterbox (noun, 13th Century English, Latin-Old English) someone who talks a lot

nickname (noun, 15th Cent. English) (1) the short *or* familiar form of a person's name, (2) an extra, special name

to conform (verb, Latin-French) to do what other people want you to do, to follow orders

to come into contact with (phrase) to meet

to compete (verb, Latin) to try to do better than other people

to interfere (verb, Latin-French) to try to influence someone *or* to tell someone else what to do

Taoist (noun, Chinese) someone who follows "The Way" – an ancient Chinese philosophy of how to see the world and how to behave

Yin and Yang (nouns, Chinese) the idea that one can see the world *and* the universe as being influenced by two opposing forces, i.e. yin = negative (-), yang = positive (+)

Memory 29

to publish (verb, Latin-French) to produce books, music and other printed matter so that they can be sold

N.C.O. (noun: non commissioned officer) a corporal *or* sergeant in the army *or* air force, i.e. the lowest level *or* rank of officers

invasion (noun, Latin) the act of entering and attacking another country

to be involved (verb, Latin) to be interested in *or* work at doing something

to check (verb, Persian-Arabic-French) to examine; to look at something to see if it is correct

electronic equipment (noun, Greek-Latin, French) things which need to use electricity in order to work, run *or* function

radar (noun, 'radio detecting and ranging', 20th Cent. English) equipment showing the movement of aircraft, ships etc.

senior (adj., Latin) older *or* higher in rank and more important

colleague (noun, Latin-French) a fellow worker

development (noun, French) the act of improving something, i.e. making it better

to maintain (verb, Latin-French) to state *or* to have a strong opinion

to seek (sought, sought) (verb, Old English) to look for, to try to find something

dominance (noun, Latin) control, having power over something else

effective (adj., Latin) working well *and* providing the correct result

to enable (verb, Latin?) to make something possible

squadron (noun, Italian) a group of air force planes

directly (adv., Latin) straight, without turning to the left or to the right

proud (adj., Latin-French-Old English) feeling pleased and happy because you or someone else has done well

to survive (verb, Latin-French) to stay *or* remain alive

Memory 30

weapon (noun, Old English) an instrument which is used for fighting

popularly (adv., Latin) generally, widely, thought *or* done by most people

to run out (verb, Old English) some kind of material comes to an end *and* there is no more of it

to plunge (verb, Latin-French) to move quickly *and* violently

destruction (noun, Latin) the act of destroying things, when something causes a great deal of harm *or* damage

to keep on going (phrase) to continue, to not stop one's movement

to cut out (verb, Norse?) to stop, to cease

to crouch down (verb, French) to squat, to bend one's knees in order to come closer to the ground

Town Hall (noun, Old English) the building which is the centre of a town government

evacuation (noun, Latin) when people leave a place of danger and go to a place which is safer

papers (noun, Latin) documents, official forms

CHAPTER 3

Memory 1

rook (noun, Old English) a kind of large bird with black feathers

to roost (verb, Old English) to rest *or* sleep on the branch of a tree

to enclose (verb, Latin-French) to surround land with a wall, hedge *or* fence

estate (noun, Latin-French) a large piece of land which belongs to one family

to skirt (verb, Norse) to form the edge of *or* to go around the edge of something

to cease (verb, Latin-French) to stop, to come to the end

Memory 2

massive (adj., French) large *and* heavy

to consist of (verb, Latin) to be made of

bedridden (adj., Old English) needing to stay in bed all the time

pantry (noun, Latin-French) a small room *or* cupboard in which to keep food and kitchen equipment

scullery (noun, Latin-French) a small room *or* part of the kitchen where kitchen equipment is kept and some of the housework is done

squeaky (adj., Swedish?) making a high-pitched noise like a mouse
communal (adj., French) belonging to a group of people

Memory 3

churn (noun, Old English) a large container for holding milk
tanker (noun, Gujarati) a lorry for carrying liquids such as oil *or* milk
depot (noun, Latin-French) a storehouse *or* warehouse
distributors (noun, Latin) people who take newspapers, food and other
    goods to places where they can be sold
dairy (noun, Old English) a place where milk is made into cream, butter
    and cheese

Memory 4

homesick (adj., Old English) feeling sad *or* unhappy because one is far
    from home
task (noun, Latin-French) a piece of work, a job of work to be done
ceramic (adj., Greek) being made of clay
milk churn (noun, Old English) a large container for holding milk
ladle (noun, Old English) a large spoon with a long handle and a large
    bowl which is made for serving liquids, e.g. a soup ladle
sapling (noun, Old English) a young tree
to trim (verb, Old English) to cut pieces off something in order to make
    it look neat
twig (noun, Old English) a small branch on a bush *or* tree
to carve (verb, Old English) to cut something in order to give it shape
    or form
to split (verb, Dutch) to cut *or* break something into two pieces
slit (noun, Old English) a long, narrow cut
to twist (verb, Old English) to wind *or* turn something around
shaft (noun, Old English) a long, narrow rod
vertically (adv., Latin) in an upright direction, straight up into the air
to crack (verb, Old English) to break *or* split open

Memory 5

estate (noun, Latin-French) a large piece of land which belongs to one family

Canon (noun, Latin-French) a priest who belongs to a cathedral

residence (noun, Latin) one's house *or* home, the place where one resides *or* lives

vicarage (noun, Latin-French) the house of a vicar, i.e. a clergyman *or* priest

to consist of (verb, Latin) to be made of

entirely (adv., Latin-French) completely, wholly, without exception

cottage (noun, Old English) a small house, often in the countryside

isolated (adj., Latin-Italian) alone, solitary, all by itself

premises (noun, Latin-French) a piece of land together with its buildings

to include (verb, Latin) to contain, to have something as part of a group

to tend to (verb, Latin-French) to have the custom that…, to often do something

vicinity (noun, Latin) surroundings, neighbourhood, the area which is nearby

to purchase (verb, French) to buy

Memory 6

to get into trouble with (phrase) to make someone angry *or* unhappy because you have done something wrong

to tell off (verb, Old English) to scold *or* complain about someone's behaviour, to tell someone that he or she has made you angry *or* unhappy

to scold (verb, Norse) to tell someone that he or she has done something wrong

to congregate (verb, Latin) the act of meeting together as a group of people

to abut (verb, French) when two things come together end to end

to top (verb, Old English) to put something on top of something else

copestone (noun, French?, Old English) a stone which is placed on top of a wall

flint stone (noun, Old English) a kind of grey-black stone that occurs in chalk, and in the past was often used to help make walls and buildings

brick (noun, French) a block of hard clay used to make houses and other buildings

cement (noun, Latin-French) a material which can help to stick bricks together

to be weathered (verb, Old English) to be changed and worn away by the action of the sun, wind, rain, ice *or* snow

to block (verb, Dutch-French) to stop *or* prevent something from moving forward

to indulge in (verb, Greek?- Latin) to do something that one enjoys

foothold (noun, Old English) a place where one can put one's foot when climbing

handhold (noun, Old English) a place where one can put one's hand when climbing

Memory 7

homesick (adj., Old English) feeling sad *or* unhappy because one is far from home

to extend (verb, Latin) to stretch something further

extended holiday (noun, Latin, Old English) a holiday which is longer than usual

to combine (verb, Latin) to join two or more things together

repeatedly (adv., Latin-French) more than once, several times, over and over again

goodies (noun, Old English) things which are tasty, good to eat

to develop (verb, French) to make, to create, to bring about

to snatch (verb, 13ᵗʰ Cent. English) to take something very quickly, to grab

to distract (verb, Latin) to make people change what they are looking at so that they look elsewhere

enforced (adj., Latin-French) having been made *or* forced to do something

Memory 8

comparatively (adv., Latin-French) rather, quite, fairly; relatively

edible (adj., Latin) fit *or* able to be eaten

establishment (noun, Latin-French) a household *or* a place of residence

decade (noun, Greek-Latin-French) a period of ten years – one after the other

herd (noun, Old English) a group of mammals which live and feed together

clumsy (adj., Swedish?) lacking skill when moving, not moving different parts of the body together

public house, pub (noun, Latin, Old English) a building with a bar *or* bars for selling alcoholic drinks

treat (noun, French) a specially pleasant *and* enjoyable occasion

to sample (verb, Latin) to try *or* take something in order to find out what it is like

evacuee (noun, Latin) someone who leaves a place of danger in order to go to a safer place

Memory 9

to mention (verb, Latin-French) to speak about something briefly, to refer to something

railings (noun, Latin-French) a kind of fence which is made of rods that are joined together

frontage (noun, Latin) the front part *or* façade of a building

adequate (adj., Latin) good enough *or* sufficient for a purpose

individual (adj., Latin) single, separate

blotter (noun, German? Dutch?) a piece of special paper which can soak up ink

to smudge (verb, German?) to smear *or* make something unclear

memorable (adj., Latin) easy to remember, worth remembering

heavy going (adj., Old English) difficult to do

Memory 10

juice (noun, Latin-French) liquid that comes from the fruit of some plants

encyclopaedia (noun, Greek-Latin) a book, often in a set of books, which gives information in alphabetical (ABC) order about many different things

ecclesiastical (adj., Greek-Latin) to do with the Christian church

medieval (adj., Latin) to do with the Middle Ages in Europe

tier (noun, French) a row, layer *or* level

phase (noun, Greek-Latin) a special time, period or stage, e.g. the changing shapes of the moon

mechanism (noun, Latin) part of a machine

moat (noun, French) a wide ditch *or* trench which is filled with water in order to protect a palace, castle, etc.

Memory 11

...have stuck in my memory (phrase) are still in my mind

science fiction (noun, Latin-French, Latin) imaginative stories which use modern ideas about science and technology

rapping (noun, Swedish?) a kind of fast, musical talking

to improvise (verb, Latin-Italian-French) to perform *or* make something quickly without planning it previously *or* beforehand

rhyming (adj., French) having similar sounds at the end of the final words of lines of poetry

prose (noun, Latin-French) spoken *or* written language which is not poetry

to imitate (verb, Latin) to copy, to do something in the same *or* similar way as something else

drivel (noun, Old English) foolish *or* silly talk *or* speech

proudly (adv., Latin-French-Old English) pleased about how well someone is doing

to involve (verb, Latin) to be concerned with

detail (noun, French) a small part of something much bigger

spindle-legged (adj., Old English, Norse) having very long, thin legs

privy (noun, Latin-French) a small toilet, especially in an outhouse *or* shed

so much so that (phrase) with the result that, and so

fearsome (adj., Old English) frightening, causing fear

barely visible (phrase) difficult to see, far away, distant

to venture (verb, Latin-French) to go to a place which is dangerous

spider-infested (adj., Old English, Latin) full of spiders, having many spiders

to linger (verb, Old English) to be slow to leave a place

Memory 12

chatterbox (see Chapter 2 Memory 28)

prone to (adj., Latin) likely to, doing something quite often

annual (noun, Latin) a book which is published once every year

in its own right (phrase) to be as good as something else, equivalent to

serial story (noun, Latin, Latin-French) a story which is published *or* presented in separate parts

funnel (noun, Latin-Provençal) a large tube *or* smokestack which carries away the smoke on a steamship

ocean (noun, Greek-Latin-French) a very large sea

liner (noun, Old English) a passenger ship

to survive (verb, Latin-French) to stay *or* remain alive

fictional (adj., Latin) not true, to do with stories which come from someone's imagination

account (noun, French) a story

Memory 13

combination (noun, Latin) two or more things which are joined together into one unit

subject matter (noun, Latin) the main *or* chief idea

to appeal to (verb, Latin-French) to interest, to be interesting *and* attractive

to feature (verb, Latin) to make something stand out *or* be important in a story

climax (noun, Greek-Latin) the most important part of a story

to track down (verb, French) to follow and then find something *or* someone

Robinson Crusoe (1719) written by Daniel Defoe (?1660-1731), this novel tells the story of a sailor who was left alone on an isolated island after his ship had hit some rocks and yet still managed to stay alive

shipwrecked (adj., Old English) to be without one's ship because it has sunk *or* been destroyed

Memory 14

to attend (verb, Latin-French) to be present at, to take part in a meeting

sociable (adj., Latin-French) friendly, happy to be with other people

opponent (noun, Latin) someone who is playing *or* fighting against another person

tremendously (adv., Latin) very much

mental (adj., Latin) to do with the mind *or* brain

skill (noun, Norse) special ability, the ability to do something very well

partner (noun, Latin-French) someone who is on the same side as another in a card game

dealer (noun, Old English) the person who gives out the cards in a card game

clockwise (adv., Latin-Dutch, Old English) in the same directions as the hands of a clock move around the dial

object (noun, Latin) an aim *or* purpose, what one wants to achieve

to consist (verb, Latin) to be made of

suit (noun, French) one of the four sets of playing cards which are used in Europe

to rank (verb, French) to put things into the order of their importance *or* power

to triumph (verb, Greek-Latin-French) to win a victory *or* to be successful

Memory 15

to celebrate (verb, Latin) to do *or* undertake special activities in order to remind people of a special event *or* happening

decorations (noun, Latin) ornaments, things which make something look more attractive than before

in advance (adv., Latin-French) beforehand, before something else is due to happen

artificial (adj., Latin) man-made, not natural

Boxing Day (noun, 19th Cent. English) this is always a holiday; at one time it was the custom to give boxes of presents to young workers on this day

to scoop (verb, German-Dutch) to lift up as if in a shovel, spoon *or* ladle

to pat (verb, 14th Cent. English) to hit something with the palm *or* flat of the hand

clasp knife (noun, Old English) a large knife with one or more blades which can fold into the handle

injury (noun, Latin) a hurt *or* harm to one's body

Memory 16

unwelcome (adj., Old English) not wanted

surprise (noun, Latin-French) something which is not expected

to snap (verb, German? Dutch?) to break suddenly

awful (adj., Norse) nasty *or* ugly

mishap (noun, Greek, Norse) an accident

blade (noun, Old English) the part of a knife which cuts *or* has the cutting edge

index finger (noun, Latin, Old English) the finger next to the thumb, with which one points

joint (noun, Latin-French) where two bones come together in a skeleton

to bleed (bled, bled) (verb, Old English) to lose blood from one's body

to bandage (verb, French) to tie a piece *or* strip of material around a wound *or* injury

to stick (stuck, stuck) (verb, Old English) to join one thing to another so that they do not separate *or* come apart

to remove (verb, Latin-French) to take something away

squeamish (adj., 15ᵗʰ Cent. unknown) when one is shocked easily by seeing blood

to waste time (phrase) to do something very slowly

to rip (verb, Flemish?) to pull something quickly *and* violently

faint (adj., French) not clear, not easy to see *or* hear

scar (noun, Greek-Latin) the mark left on one's skin after a wound has healed

Memory 17

to baptise (verb, Greek-Latin) to drop water onto a baby's head in church in order to show that it is now a Christian

to christen (verb, Hebrew-Greek-Latin-Old English) to give someone a Christian name when he *or* she is baptised

duty (noun, French) something which one must do as part of one's place in society

responsible (adj., Latin) to have control of *or* to be in charge of something

faith (noun, Latin-French) a strong belief in something

religious (adj., Latin-French) believing in God

expectation (noun, Latin) a requirement *or* something which must be done

pure (adj., Latin-French) morally well-behaved *and* not doing bad things

devout (adj., Latin-French) very religious

demure (adj., French?) quiet *and* modest, not boasting *or* 'showing off'

to pump (verb, Spanish?-Dutch) to push air into something by moving a handle

hymn (noun, Greek-Latin) a religious song

lever (noun, Latin-French) a bar which is fixed at one point *and* can be moved up and down *or* from side to side in order to move something else

dial (noun, Latin) something like a card with marks on it to measure *or* show how far something else has moved

needle (noun, Old English) a thin piece of metal with a point

choir (noun, Latin-French) a group of singers

choirboy (noun, Latin-French, 14th Cent. English) a boy who sings in a church choir

activity (noun, Latin) what one does *or* when one is moving

I owe my love of music to... (phrase) I love music because of...

chorister (noun, Latin) a singer in a choir

uniform (noun, Latin) clothes showing that one is part of a special group
cassock (noun, Italian-French) a piece of long black clothing which is worn by priests
surplice (noun, Latin-French) a piece of priests' clothing which reaches to the knees
angelic (adj., Greek-Latin-Old English) like an angel, i.e. a heavenly being

Memory 18

to encourage (verb, Latin-French) to help someone to feel better about doing something
competition (noun, Latin) people trying to do better than each other
prayer (noun, Latin-French) a spoken *or* written message to God
hymn (noun, Greek-Latin) a religious song
congregation (noun, Latin) a group of people who come together in church
to prefer (verb, Latin) to like one thing better than another
Canon (noun, Latin-French) a priest who belongs to a cathedral
to require (verb, Latin-French) to order, to tell someone to do something
collect (noun, Latin) a short prayer for use in a church service
to be connected (verb, Latin) to be linked to, associated with, related to something
needless to say (phrase) of course, it is a fact that..., it is true that...
to remind (verb, Old English) to cause someone to remember something
lych gate (noun, Old English) the roofed gate to a churchyard where the coffin was kept for a short time during a funeral
porch (noun, Latin-French) a small roofed shelter at the doorway to a house *or* church
to gather (verb, Old English) to bring together into a group
to bother to... (verb, Irish?) to take time *or* trouble to do something, to

concern oneself with

to recite (verb, Latin) to say something from memory, i.e. without looking at a text

to persuade (verb, Latin) to speak to someone so that he *or* she does what you want

mental effort (noun, Latin, Latin-French) using one's brain *or* mind

Memory 19

Prime Minister (noun, Latin, Latin-French) the head of the government in parliament

Winston Churchill (1874-1965) a politician and leader of Great Britain during World War II

to announce (verb, Latin-French) to say, to state, to tell people something

rocket (noun, Italian-French) a weapon which can fly high into the air and then explode when it hits the ground

she wasted no time (phrase) she acted quickly

unexpected (adj., Latin) something which happens when one does not know that it is going to happen

life style (noun, Old English, Latin) a way of living, culture, one's beliefs and habits

timing (noun, Old English) choosing the time to do something

term (noun, Latin-French) part of a school year: England has three terms per year with a holiday of several weeks between each one

primary (adj., Latin) the first stage of English education

valuable (adj., Latin-French) worthwhile, having great value

to adapt (verb, Latin) to change oneself in order to suit *or* fit changing conditions

relationships (noun, Latin) the connections between different people

circumstances (noun, Latin-French) the situation, surroundings *or* conditions in which one finds oneself

formative period (noun, Latin-French, Greek-Latin) a time when one learns new things and therefore changes into a new person

to celebrate (verb, Latin) to do *or* undertake special activities in order to remind people of a special event

to organise (verb, Greek-Latin-French) to arrange, to put things into a good order

firework (noun, Old English) something containing gunpowder which, when lit, will explode in order to provide bright colours, loud noises and entertainment

party (noun, Latin-French) a group of people who come together in order to have fun and enjoy themselves

patch (noun, French) a small flat piece of something

air-raid shelter (see Chapter Two Memory 18)

pyrotechnics (noun, Greek) a display of fireworks

random (adj., French) without any order, not following a pattern

to provide (verb, Latin) to give

glorious (adj., Latin-French) brilliantly beautiful

Memory 20

connection (noun, Latin) a link, a relationship

to deem (verb, Old English) to believe, think, consider

occasion (noun, Latin) the time when something happens

to greet (verb, Old English) to meet someone and say "Hullo!"

to make money (phrase) to get money by working in business *or* by trading

illegal (adj., Latin) not lawful, against the law

trading (noun, 14th Cent. English) buying and selling things

to associate with (verb, Latin) to link *or* connect two things together in one's mind

evacuation (noun, Latin) when people leave a place of danger and go to a safer place

wheel chair (noun, Old English, Latin-French) a special chair mounted on large wheels and used to carry people who cannot walk

fête (noun, French) a kind of party, often in the open air, with various tables offering food and entertainment

to guess (verb, Swedish?) to decide something with little or no knowledge to help you

weight (noun, Old English) a measure of how heavy something is

competition (noun, Latin) an activity where people try to do better than each other

joint winner (noun, Latin-French, Old English) each person who gets a prize when there is more than one winner

to share (verb, Old English) to join one or more other people in getting something

accurately (adv., Latin) precisely, without a mistake *or* an error

luxury (noun, Latin-French) something rare *and/or* expensive

Memory 21

seaside resort (noun, Old English, French) a town by the sea which people like to visit

sojourn (noun, Latin-French) staying somewhere *or* residing for a short time

tide (noun, Old English) the rise and fall of the sea level caused by the pull of the sun and the moon

to ebb (verb, Old English) to flow back, i.e. the sea goes away from the shore

expanse (noun, Latin) a large flat, area

donkey (noun, 18th Cent. English) an ass, long-eared member of the horse family

to be steadied (verb, Old English) to be held firmly

in charge (phrase) in control, in command

string (noun, Old English) a line of things one after the other

starting point (noun, Old English, Latin-French) the place from where something comes

exploration trip (noun, Latin, French) a journey made in order to find *or* discover new places

occasional (adj., Latin) not frequent, from time to time, not occurring often

to consume (verb, Latin) to eat *or* drink

I have the feeling that (phrase) I believe that...

guest house (noun, Old English) a private house which offers accommodation to travellers and other paying guests

Memory 22

limestone (noun, Old English) a kind of rock made from the remains of dead sea animals

geology (noun, Greek) the scientific study of the history and structure of the earth

favours the creation of (phrase) helps to make, leads to the making of

cave (noun, Latin-French) a large hole under the ground *or* inside a hill

evacuee (noun, Latin) someone who leaves a place of danger and goes to a safer place

column (noun, Latin) an upright post *or* pillar

strange (adj., Latin-French) odd, unusual, not normal *or* peculiar

forbidding (adj., Old English) unfriendly *or* dangerous

to ignore (verb, Latin) to take no notice of, to disregard

silent (adj., Latin) having no noise *or* sound

eerie (adj., 13th Cent. Scottish) frightening *and* strange, mysterious

rock formation (noun, French, Latin-French) the shape *or* form of some rocks

witch (noun, Old English) someone, usually a woman, who practises magic

magic (noun, Greek-French) the use of spells in order to obtain supernatural power

fête (noun, French) a kind of village party with several tables which offer food and entertainment

conjuror (noun, Latin-French) someone who performs tricks which seem impossible

wand (noun, Norse) a rod

flag (noun, 16ᵗʰ Cent., unknown) a piece of cloth with a design *or* pattern which represents a country, state etc.

objects (noun, Latin) things

to perform (verb, French) to do something *or* carry out entertainment

card trick (noun, Latin-French) an activity *or* something done with playing cards which seems like magic

conjuring tricks (noun, Latin-French) activities done for entertainment which seem like magic

Memory 23

reading between the lines (phrase) finding the meaning of something which is not actually said *or* written

nostalgia (noun, Greek) looking back to happy times

golden period (noun, Old English, Greek-Latin) a happy length of time

connections (noun, Latin) links, relationships

presumably (adv., Latin-French) one can believe it, it seems likely that

coffin (noun, Latin-French) the box which is used to hold a corpse (dead body)

briefly (adv., Latin-French) for a short time

wedding (noun, Old English) the act *or* ceremony of getting married

excursion (noun, Latin) a short journey to a special place – and back again

to be fond of (verb, 14ᵗʰ Cent. English) to like something *or* someone very much

to prepare (verb, Latin) to get ready for an activity

Advanced Level Examinations these national tests for school pupils took place in the last year of secondary education when the pupils were aged 18

to go into service (phrase) to become a household servant, e.g. a nursemaid, nanny

Memory 24

to imagine (verb, Latin-French) to think, believe *or* guess

to reside (verb, Latin) to live, *or* dwell in one particular place

mansion (noun, Latin-French) a very large house belonging to rich people

humble (adj., Latin-French) not important socially, not high-class

decade (noun, Latin-French) a period of ten years one after another

maternal (adj., Latin) to do with one's mother

tenant (noun, Latin-French) someone who rents property and pays money to a landlord *or* landowner

employee (noun, Latin-French) someone who is paid to work for someone else

infant (noun, Latin) a very young child

vice admiral (noun, Latin, Arabic-Latin-French) the officer who is second in command of a fleet of warships

naval (adj., Latin-French) to do with the navy, i.e. a country's warships

to sink (sank, sunk) verb, Old English) to drop down *or* descend into a liquid such as water

a spectacular success (phrase) an extremely good result

to drive (drove, driven) (verb, Old English) to travel by car *or* a similar vehicle

ancestral (adj., Latin-French) to do with one's ancestors, i.e. the former members of one's family

Memory 25

trench (noun, Latin-French) a ditch which is dug in order to provide protection

203

childless (adj., Old English) without any children

bearing the name (phrase) called, having the name

descendants (noun, Latin-French) people who descend, i.e. follow on, from former members of their family

to turn one's mind towards (phrase) to think about

progression (noun, Latin) the changing *or* going forward - from one step to another

generations (noun, Latin) the different levels of a family, i.e. parents, grandparents, children and grandchildren

accidental (adj., Latin-French) happening by chance, not deliberate, not on purpose

to switch (verb, Dutch?) to change two things around, to swap, to exchange one thing for another

name tag (noun, Old English, unknown) a piece *or* strip of something with one's name on it

parasite (noun, Greek-Latin) an animal *or* plant which lives in *or* on another from which it gets its food

to bear the brunt (verb, Old English, unknown) to do most of the work

to count something as (phrase) to consider, to decide that, to judge

Memory 26

in contact with (phrase) part of

evident (adj., Latin) easy to see *or* understand

to exploit (verb, Latin-French) to use, to make use of

resources (noun, Latin-French) things which people can use, e.g. other people, land, minerals etc.

exhausted (adj., Latin) tired out, with resources at an end *or* finished

to demand (verb, Latin-French) to request *or* ask for something very strongly

independence (noun, Latin-French) freedom from others, the ability to govern *or* control one's own country

post-war (adj., Latin, French) after the war

to exist (verb, Latin) to be

to revert to (verb, Latin) to return *or* change back to

insignificant (adj., Latin-French) unimportant

unwilling (adj., Old English) not wanting to do something, wanting to avoid

to recognise (verb, Latin) to accept an idea, to admit

grossly overcrowded (phrase, Latin-French, Old English) having too many people in one area

...we were living on borrowed time (clause) we did not have much time left to correct our mistakes and to solve our problems

guilty (adj., Old English) in the wrong, having behaved badly

Little Englander: a politician or historian who believes that England is not a great and important country

on the contrary (phrase) not at all, quite the reverse, the opposite is true

inventor (noun, Latin) someone who creates new ideas *or* machines etc.

innovator (noun, Latin) someone who begins to use new machines *or* introduces new ideas

to be handicapped (verb, 17th Cent. English) to suffer from a disadvantage, to be made weaker in some way

bubble (noun, Scandinavian?) a thin film of liquid which forms a hollow globe around air or gas, e.g. a soap bubble

burst (burst, burst) (verb, Old English) to break open suddenly, to explode

the bubble has burst (sentence) what was very good has now disappeared

Punctuation Exercises

Choose a passage and copy it out using standard punctuation. Then compare your work with the original Memory.

Sometimes more than one answer is possible!

Chapter One   Memory 4

i also never knew my maternal grandmother because she died on 9th may 1932 at the age of 57 her maiden name was lydia hartnell bishop taylor and she was born on 14th august 1874 into a chemists family in leicester she was presumably a middle class person but it seems that her father took to drink and his family then experienced financial difficulties lydia who was also known as lillie became some sort of servant at a mansion in dinder near wells in somerset my grandfather cyril randall met her when he worked there as a groom and they were married in 1907 at st matthews church fulham cyril now worked as a tram driver and conductor and so just like my other grandfather changed his job from handling horses to being involved with mechanised transport unlike joseph meadows who eventually lived in a relatively rural area in essex cyril randall chose to move from the countryside to the big city london for a while he and his wife lived in fulham first of all at 15 cranbury road and then at 50 rosebury road at some time after 1908 he moved his family across the river thames to 115a aslett street wandsworth after his first wife died in 1932 and my mother left home in 1935 he married alma one of his nieces and moved to 3 colman court kimber road southfields sw 18 he lived in this block of flats with his second wife and their son david for the rest of his life

Chapter One   Memory 12

i know very little about my fathers family i dont know whether joseph meadows was an only child or whether he had siblings he may have had one or more brothers and or sisters but my father didnt tell me much about his back ground i can only assume that my paternal ancestors came from east anglia i know far more about my mothers family because i inherited the randall family bible this was given to mary henrietta randall by her mother presumably when her daughter married george randall in 1880 or thereabouts i have the birth certificate of mary henrietta whose maiden name was oatley she was born on 30th may 1856 and she came from dulcote which is the first village heading east out of the cathedral city of wells in somerset she was baptised on 6th july 1856 and died on 21st october 1945 aged 89 her father edmund or edward oatley was a farm labourer and her mother whose maiden name was amelia webb couldnt write her name but needed to sign her name by making a cross i also have the birth certificate of george randall he was born on 5th august 1861 in the village of merriott near crewkerne in the south of somerset he died on 11th january 1927 at the age of 65 his fathers name was given as john rendall a farm labourer and his mothers maiden name was mary ann trask like amelia webb she also made a cross because she couldnt sign her name it seems that a century before i was born most of my ancestors lived and worked on the land

Chapter Two   Memory 6

the victor house flats ran parallel to and were set back from oakleigh road this main road ran approximately east west up a gentle hill for a mile until it reached a cross roads at whetstone here it joined the a1000 otherwise known as the great north road which ran northwards to barnet and then led all the way to york and on to edinburgh whetstone was an important shopping centre for my mother i can still remember the sainsburys store which was on the left hand side of the a1000 as we faced barnet in the 1940s this grocers shop still had a marble topped cheese counter with large cheeses which were cut into pieces with a fine steel wire there were several counters each with its special range of foods and so my mother and i had to queue several times in order to fill our shopping bag there was a short service road in front of our flats and on the opposite north side of oakleigh road there was another parade of shops and flats these were only two storeys high what they lacked in height however they made up for in length since there were ten shops under the flats directly opposite our flat was a confectioners and tobacconists shop which was run by mrs carminati and her italian husband the latter died in january 1944 they lived in the flat above the shop next to the carminatis running eastwards were a greengrocers shop a grocers shop and then a dress shop after this there were a hardware shop a barbers shop three more shops and then a fish and chip shop which included a restaurant beyond these was a combined petrol station and repair garage

Chapter Two   Memory 12

the radio also provided an important form of home entertainment i can still remember listening to a weekly comedy programme as we ate our sunday lunch it was called itma its that man again and provided our countrymen with a patriotic morale boost in the war against hitler even as an infant i knew that the humour was very weak but it made us feel a bit happier there was very little plot story and much of the programme consisted of catch phrases mrs mopp mop the cleaning lady would say can i do you now sir and an army officer colonel chin strap when offered an alcoholic drink would say i dont mind if i do there was also a german spy funf fünf = 5 in german who used to say this is funf speaking i go i come back the actors were assisted by lots of sound effects such as the sounds of doors opening papers being shuffled and things falling on the floor these sound effects made the scenes come alive and helped to disguise the fact that they werent really very funny one advantage of listening to the radio was that i could do other things while listening to it another advantage was that it encouraged me to use my imagination a third advantage was that i often listened to light classical music without being aware that i was increasing my musical knowledge it was only when i came to re read my diaries that i realised how important the radio had been to me until i left home to do my national service at the age of eighteen the radio was never so important to me again

Chapter Three   Memory 13

my parents came to see me for the first time during the week end of friday 29th september after that my mother had to come alone because my father worked on saturday mornings and couldnt take time off work on that saturday my mother and i went into wells and while there we visited the bookshop which was on the right hand side half way down the hill from the town square she bought two books for me rudkin and a gang of ten which i still have on a shelf in my study they were both hard back books their covers were a combination of card board and linen and i still think that books with linen covers are beautiful because of the pattern of the cloth rudkin had been published by frederick muller in 1938 and my copy was a second edition from 1943 i know nothing about the authoress yvonne wingfield king but i really enjoyed this imaginative fairy story which included lots of pictures and twenty eight poems i found a gang of ten more difficult to read perhaps because its subject matter didnt appeal to me so much at that time it had been published by secker and warburg in the usa in 1942 and was then published in england in january 1944 my copy was from the second edition of march 1944 it featured a group of children of different nationalities who came together in a town in california they included boys from new york norway england russia and holland girls from france and china and there was also a young woman journalist from washington the climax of the book was reached when they tracked down and caught two nazi spies apart from these two books and the old fashioned annual i also found a copy of robinson crusoe in the cottage i enjoyed reading this so much that i some times pretended that my bed in the big bed room was a raft or a ship and played at being ship wrecked

Chapter Three Memory 23

it is easy to see reading between the lines that i look back at my time in dinder with nostalgia despite the war time conditions it was a golden period for me but all good things must come to an end and my close connections with somerset became weaker after auntie margaret died of her illness on 25th february 1947 my mother took me to bristol with auntie may in order to meet auntie rose margarets funeral took place on saturday 1st march presumably at dinder church but i couldnt bring myself to look at her in her coffin because i was frightened of what i might see never having seen a dead body before it was enough to have the memory of her as she had been auntie may visited us at whetstone that summer and then on 29th july took me back with her to dinder where i stayed until 2nd september that was almost the end of my connection with dinder because i spent my 1948 and 1949 holidays at pitsea i did return briefly a few more times in august 1950 my parents and i stayed at the cottage for three days and then returned two weeks later in order to attend the wedding of joan randall and william warner at burnham the next year we went to swanage for our summer holiday and while there made an excursion to dinder on tuesday 7th august it was fortunate that we were able to see auntie may on that occasion because she died three years later in 1954 my mother told me that she had always been fond of her and that they had gone to the theatre together several times before my mother got married my final visit to the cottage was in april 1955 when i was preparing for my a levels advanced level examinations we were there for only three nights my parents returned in july 1956 by which time i was in the army that was their final visit thirty one years after their first visit together because auntie rose went back into service with mrs gilroy and the cottage was eventually sold